Anonymous

Sketches and Incidents

A Budget from the Saddle-Bags of a Superannuated Itinerant

Anonymous

Sketches and Incidents
A Budget from the Saddle-Bags of a Superannuated Itinerant

ISBN/EAN: 9783337098025

Printed in Europe, USA, Canada, Australia, Japan

Cover: Foto ©ninafisch / pixelio.de

More available books at **www.hansebooks.com**

SKETCHES & INCIDENTS;

OR,

A BUDGET FROM THE SADDLE-BAGS

OF A

SUPERANNUATED ITINERANT.

VOLUME I.

GEORGE PECK, EDITOR.

Cincinnati:
PUBLISHED BY A. POE & L. HITCHCOCK,
FOR THE METHODIST EPISCOPAL CHURCH, AT THE WESTERN BOOK
CONCERN, CORNER OF MAIN AND EIGHTH STREETS.

R. P. THOMPSON, PRINTER.
1862.

Entered, according to Act of Congress, in the year 1845 by
G. LANE & C. B. TIPPETT, in the Clerk's Office of the District
Court of the Southern District of New-York.

PREFACE.

In order to give the following sketches a slight aspect of unity, the author has adopted an arrangement which he hopes will not detract in the most scrupulous estimation from the general veracity of the work.

Though adapted to the Sunday-School Library, it is chiefly designed for the advanced youth of the church; and the author would not dissemble that, in his matter and in his style, he has studied to meet the wants of this interesting class. While our denominational literature abounds in standard works for adults, and includes an excellent series for Sunday schools, it is comparatively destitute of such productions as have been furnished to the youth of the Calvinistic portion of the religious community, by Robert Philip, the Messrs. Abbot, &c. The present publication, though of a widely different character, will be acceptable, it is hoped, to the same class of readers. Perhaps its more fragmentary form may serve its object. The author has sought to convey in these sketches important lessons, and to excite an affection for the character and institutions of the church. A few of them have already been extensively circulated in the religious prints. The interest which they have thus excited has encouraged their publication in the present form.

CONTENTS.

	Page
Introduction	7
Old Jeddy. There's Rest at Home	9
Wesley's Character	18
A Vision in the Wilderness	28
Children of Religious Parents	35
The Duel	42
Bishop Asbury	51
Presentiments	58
Anecdotes of Jesse Lee	63
The Moral Sublime	71
The Converted Dutchman	76
Dr. Coke	81
Progress in Piety	86
Black Harry of St. Eustatius	94
The Way of Life	102
Origin of Methodist Economy	113
Adaptation of Methodism to our Country	120
The Hospitable Widow and the Tract	126
My Library	131
Mighty Men	142
Jack and his Master	151
Religious Cheerfulness	155
Too Late	161

INTRODUCTION.

It pleased God early to honor the writer of these pages with a place in the itinerant ranks of the Methodist Episcopal Church. His travels have been extensive, imposing a little hard service, and affording many interesting recollections. It has been his happiness to know many of the fathers who composed the first itinerant band, the *legio tonans* (thundering legion) of the American church. Infirmities have compelled him to retire from the field; his war-horse sleeps under the sod of a distant prairie, and his shattered trumpet gives but a feeble and occasional note. His saddle-bags remain. They hang in his study before him while penning these lines; he can never part with them. They are fuller of eminiscences than ever they were of anything else, and if God will, he wishes them placed under his head as a pillow when dying. To beguile the tedium of retirement and illness, he has written the following sketches, chiefly incidents of ministerial life. As they were written they were deposited in his old saddle-bags until they accumulated to a considerable budget. They are now brought forth and presented to the reader: if they should afford him a lesson of warning or consolation, if they should produce one impression which shall survive the grave, the writer will be rewarded and thankful.

SKETCHES AND INCIDENTS:

OLD JEDDY—THERE'S REST AT HOME.

' *There remaineth, therefore, a rest for the people of God.*"—Paul.

I WAS preaching one Sunday afternoon in tha door of a log cabin in the village of P———, to a congregation which filled the house and the front yard. When about half through the sermon, I observed an old negro riding alone toward the house. He dismounted, fastened his horsa to a tree, and took his stand among the throng. The tears soon trickled down his furrowed cheeks, and it seemed impossible for him to repress some hearty exclamations. At the conclusion of the service he presented himself with profound reverence as my guide to Colonel M.'s, nineteen miles distant. It was my next appointment, and having just arrived on the circuit, I needed some guidance. I had already preached three times and rode twenty-three miles that day, and proposed to Jedediah, or Jeddy, as he was called, to tarry till the morning ; but he replied that his master, the colonel, insisted upon seeing me that evening. "Do go, massa," said Jeddy, "for no massa preacher be there for four months." I mounted to start, but Jeddy's horse was found too lame to return. The late rains had swept away a bridge on the only road, and rendered it necessary to take an indirect course through a boggy prairie, in order to cross the stream nearer its head. The horse had sprained one of his legs in a quicksand of this prairie, but Jeddy insisted on returning on foot.

We started into the prairie, but had not got far when I perceived that, owing to the wet state of the ground, we should not, at Jeddy's pace, reach our destination till the next morning. But, though slipping and tugging at almost every step, the good-hearted negro's large eyes gleamed with delight at the thought that he had induced the "massa preacher" to accompany him. I directed him to mount behind me: he seemed astonished at my kindness, and looked at me in silent amazement, but at last yielded to my request. By a little familiarity he became quite communicative. I led him into a recital of his whole history, particularly of his Christian experience. It was related with evident sincerity and deep emotion; the tears frequently flowed from the old man's eyes, and I could not restrain my own; we wept together like children. Though jogging along in no very interesting plight, I felt that St. Paul's language was not inapplicable to us—God " hath raised us up together, and made us sit together in heavenly places in Christ Jesus."

When we had passed the first nine miles, the night was falling fast, and, what was infinitely worse, we began to falter among those patches of quicksand so frequent and so dangerous in some of the western prairies. After plunging into a number of these, Jeddy dismounted, to relieve the danger by lessening the burden of the horse. We had not gone twenty rods further before the poor animal sunk above his knees in the mire, and only extricated himself by the utmost violence. Though accustomed to greater difficulties, the fatigues of the day had so affected me that I began to show less courage than the poor slave who guided me. Dismounting, I leaned wearily against my horse, and expressed a disposition to return rather than risk the perils and fatigues of the remaining distance.

" No, massa," replied Jeddy, " be not discouraged, there be rest at home for you "

There was something either in the tone of Jeddy's voice, or my own mood of mind, which gave the expression at once a double sense "Yes," I involuntarily exclaimed, "thank God, there is a home for us, Jeddy, where the weary are at rest."

"O yes, massa," said the old labor-worn negro, as the tears started in his eyes, " me often tinks of dat—me hopes to get dere some day."

"'There is rest at home"—the sentence gave me new energy, and has often done so since, 'n many a harder trial.

We jogged along, but ever and anon were struggling in the bogs. Wearied at last, we sat down on a small protuberance of the prairie, too fatigued to proceed.

"How old are you, Jeddy?" I inquired.

"Seventy-three, massa; me be getting toward dat 'home,' massa."

"Have you a wife, Jeddy?" "Yes, massa; but me know not where she be: former massa love not God, and sold her far away." "Have you children?" "Yes, massa." "And where are they?" "All gone, too, massa, me know not where. But we all served God, massa, and hope to meet in dat home where be rest." The tears started afresh in the old man's eyes. I could inquire no further. My feelings overpowered me. What, thought I, are my sufferings compared with those of this poor, sorrow-stricken servant of my Master!

"There is rest for us at home," said I involuntarily, and motioned to proceed. It was very dark, the rain was falling, and my horse limped with lameness. I was compelled to lead him by the bridle the remaining ten dreary miles. Through rain, and mud, and quicksands, we plodded on, nerved against them all by the thought which ever recurred with refreshing influence to my mind, that "there was rest for us at home." At last the glimmer of a distant light fell on our course. "Dat is home, massa," exclaimed Jeddy, with ecstasy.

So, I have often thought since then, gleams the light of hope over the valley and shadow of death to the Christian pilgrim.

I was received about midnight at the log cabin, wet and weary, yet as an angel of God. The table had been spread with everything good the house could afford for my refreshment. After many congratulations, a prayer and a song of praise, I laid me down to rest. *Rest*, thought I, what a sweet word! Never did I feel its significance more than in the slumbers of that night, sweetened as they were by beautiful visions of that better land where "there remaineth a *rest* for the people of God." The phrase of my aged guide wove itself into all my dreaming thoughts, and yet with such effect as not in the least to disturb my repose. At one time I thought I was reclining my head on the breast of a seraph, and dying—nay, it was falling asleep in Jesus—pervaded from head to foot with the most delicious sensations—a feeling of profound repose, which I never felt before nor since. At another I was gliding in the air, up over the hills, down into the valleys of heaven, without touching the soil, and wrapt in an unimaginable ecstasy—an ecstasy intense, and yet strangely tranquil. At another, I was sweetly sleeping under a leafy tree near one of its streams, on whose margin all varieties of flowers were bending and blushing, as if at the reflection of their own charms; and though asleep, yet it seemed that my eyes were open, drinking in all the indescribable scenery, while music, slow, sweet, and subdued by distance, flowed like a soft breeze of the south over my charmed spirit, and ever and anon a seraph glided by, smiling with unspeakable love, and uttering as he passed, "*Rest thee, brother*," and leaving behind him a very wake of fragrance like the odor of June roses. These were fantasies, but how sweet were they!

I rose the next morning with the freshness

of youth, greeted by the sweet and ever-varying notes of a mocking-bird, which had perched on a tree over my chamber.

* * * * * * *

Ten years had passed—years of much labor and sad changes in my history—when I had occasion to visit a much more remote frontier settlement. I preached in a log school-house, to a congregation gathered from within twenty miles around. At the close of the discourse, a Mr. M. introduced himself to me as the son of my former host, Colonel M. The colonel had emancipated his slaves, and during a long period of sickness was converted, and died, it was believed, the death of the righteous. The son, indulging the characteristic propensity of the family, had advanced with the frontier line, and the old colored servants, unwilling to disperse, had accompanied him, and were settled about him. One of them, he said, was not expected to live from hour to hour. We went immediately to the sick man's cabin; it was surrounded by colored people, weeping like children for a father. On a bed in a corner lay the dying man. I approached to address him; his languid eye kindled, and in a moment there was a mutual recognition. It was old Jeddy. Need I tell the reader the effect on myself and on the dying African? Leaning over the bed, and taking his hand, I asked, " Do you remember, Jeddy, the boggy prairie at ——?"

" O yes, massa; dat precious night," he replied, gasping for breath.

" Your pilgrimage is most ended. There's rest for you at home, Jeddy."

The old saint had not forgotten the phrase. His dying eye kindled anew, and in broken expressions he responded, "Yes, bless de Lord, massa, me most dere, me most home; me poor, old, weary servant, O very weary, but going home, going home." Tears of gratitude and joy expressed still more fully his thoughts. When he had nearly lost the power of speech, he continued to utter this phrase, and his last words were, " Rest—home!" He died about eleven o'clock that night, and I have no doubt that by the midnight hour he had passed through the " everlasting gates," and was hailed by seraphim amid the " excellent glory."

Often, while drooping under the fatigues and diseases of those wild regions—often, in laying my head on my saddle, to spend the night in the forest, have I recalled the phrase of Jeddy, " There's rest at home." There has been a spell of power in these words which no labor no peril, has been able to dissipate.

Minister of God, wandering to and fro, without a resting place, to seek the lost sheep of the house of Israel, art thou at times weary? Dost thou long for a home and repose? Do thy little ones die in thy absence, and are their graves scattered in the land? Cheer thee, brother, thy home is above, and a rest remaineth for thee there.

Aged pilgrim, art thou bending over thy staff, like the patriarch "seeking a better country;" do thy aged limbs tremble on the way? Be of good courage, the difficult heights before thee are the " Delectable Mountains." Struggle on; thou art on the threshold of thy home: there is rest for thee there.

Afflicted saint, is it thy lot not to do, but suffer the will of thy Lord? Art thou weary and weak, and in pains; are weeks or months of languishing before thee? "Trust thou in the Lord for ever," for thy "light afflictions" are but for a moment," compared with the "rest that remaineth" for thee. Suffer on, the end is at hand, when thou shalt "enter into his rest."

WESLEY'S CHARACTER.

"*A prince and a great man in Israel.*"—David.

I HAVE known few men who had greater ability in the discrimination of human character than Judge M.,—an ability which he had acquired as well by extensive biographical reading as by the study of life.

He had been reading Southey's Life of Wesley. "It is a most interesting production," said he, "but very unsatisfactory. Its style is a specimen of pure and vigorous English, and its materials are singularly rich, even romantic, but it lacks unity, and the final impression is vague. Some of the sketches of Wesley's 'helpers,' as they are called, would adorn the romances of chivalry; but I have received from the book no definite idea of Wesley himself."

I found, nevertheless, that the idea he had received, however indefinite, was not too favorable.

Watson's pungent and eloquent critique on Southey had just appeared. I sent it to him, accompanied with Moore's Life of Wesley. While reading them, he frequently sent to my library for other publications which were referred to by these writers, particularly the works of Wesley, Gillies, Whitefield, &c. On returning them, he expressed the interest he had felt in their perusal.

"I have never before," said he, "given so much attention to an ecclesiastical subject. Wesley's character is itself a study. To one who has not examined these works I should hesitate to express fully my estimate of him. He equaled Luther in energy and courage, while he excelled him in prudence and learning. He equaled Melancthon in learning and prudence, while he surpassed him in courage and energy; and there are few of the excellences of both the Wittemberg reformers which were not combined and transcended in his individual character.

"He possessed in an eminent degree one trait of a master mind—the power of comprehending at once the general outlines and the details of plans, the aggregate and the integrants. It is this power which forms the philosophical genius in science; it is indispensable to the successful commander and the great statesman. It is illustrated in the whole economical system of Methodism—a system which, while it fixes itself to the smallest locality with the utmost detail and tenacity, is sufficiently general in its provisions to reach the ends of the world, and still maintain its unity of spirit and discipline.

"No man knew better than Wesley the importance of small things. You recollect that his whole financial system was based on weekly penny collections; and it was a rule of his preachers never to omit a single preaching appointment, except when the 'risk of life or limb' required. So far as I can judge, he was the first to apply extensively the plan of tract distribution. He wrote, printed, and scattered over the kingdom, placards on almost every topic of morals and religion. In addition to the usual services of the church, he introduced what you call the *band meeting*, the *class meeting*, the *prayer meeting*, the *love feast*, and the *watch night*. Not content with his itinerant laborers, he called into use the less available powers of his people, by establishing the departments of *local preachers*, *exhorters*, and *leaders*. It was, in fine, by gathering together fragments, by combining minutiæ, that he formed that powerful system of spiritual means which is transcending all others in the evangelization of the world.

"It was not only in the theoretical construction of plans that Wesley excelled; he was, if possible, still more distinguished by practical energy. The variety and number of his labors would be absolutely incredible to me with less authentic evidence than that which corroborates them. He was perpetually traveling and preaching, studying and writing, translating and abridging, superintending his societies, and applying his great plans. According to one of these authors, he traveled usually *five thousand* miles a year, preaching twice and thrice a day, commencing at five o'clock in the morning; and in all this incessant traveling and preaching he carried with him the studious and meditative habits of the philosopher. No department of human inquiry was omitted by him. 'History, poetry, and philosophy,' says he, 'I read on horseback.'

"Wesley, like Luther, knew the importance of the press; he kept it teeming with his publications, and his itinerant preachers were good agents for their circulation. And here [opening one of the volumes] is a sentence addressed to them on the subject which indicates his character:—'Carry them with you through every round; exert yourselves in this; be not ashamed, be not weary, leave no stone unturned.' His works, including abridgments and translations, amounted (if I estimate rightly) to about two hundred volumes. These comprise treatises on almost every subject of divinity, poetry, music, history; natural, moral, metaphysical, and political philosophy. He wrote as he preached, *ad populum*, and he may indeed be considered the leader in those exertions which are now being made for the popular diffusion of knowledge.

"Differing from the usual character of men who are given to various exertions and many plans, he was accurate and profound. He was an adept in classical literature and the use of the classical tongues; his writings are adorned with their finest passages. He was familiar with a number of modern languages; and I consider his own style one of the best examples of strength and perspicuity among English writers. He seems to have been ready on every subject of learning and general literature. As a logician, he was remarkably clear and decisive.

"He was but little addicted to those exhilarations and contrarieties of frame which characterize imaginative minds. His temperament was warm, but not fiery. His intellect never appears inflamed, but always glowing—a serene radiance. His immense labors were accomplished, not by the impulses of restless

siasm, but by the cool calculation of his plans, and the steady self-possession with which he pursued them. I like that maxim of his—
'Though I am always in haste, I am never in a hurry.' He was as economical of his time as a miser could be of his gold; rising at four o'clock in the morning, and allotting to every hour its appropriate work. 'Leisure and I have taken leave of each other,' said he. And yet such was the happy arrangement of his employments, that amid a multiplicity which would distract an ordinary man, he declares that 'there are few persons who spend so many hours secluded from all company as myself.' The wonder of his character is the self-control by which he preserved himself calm, while he kept all in excitement around him.

"He was a contrast to Whitefield. Whitefield was born an orator. The qualities of the orator made up his whole genius; they were the first mental manifestations of his childhood, but were pent up in his heart, a magazine of energies, until kindled by the influence of religion, when they broke forth, like the fires of a volcano. He was a man of boundless soul. He was a host of generous sympathies; and every sympathy, in him, was a passion. This was, perhaps, the secret of his eloquence. The

Athenian orator said that action was eloquence. Perhaps antiquity has given undue authority to this remark. The pantomime is not eloquent; but strong passion always is, and always would be, had it the expression of neither hand nor feature, but the tremulous tones of the excited voice coming from an unseen source upon the ear. There is no eloquence without feeling Even the histrionic orator must *feel*—not affect to feel, but, by giving himself up to the illusion of reality in ideal scenes, *actually* feel. Whitefield's whole Christian course showed the prevalence of mighty feelings.

"Whitefield was no legislator: he acted entirely without a system. Here was his great defect. Had he combined the contriving powers of Wesley with his own effective eloquence, it cannot be doubted that he would have occupied the high place of the latter, or, at least, a similar position in a separate sect holding the tenets of Calvinism. His powers of address were much more immediately effective than Wesley's; and if they had been applied to the establishment of a well-organized system, as were Wesley's, the result would have been immense. He moved like a comet, dazzling and amazing the world, but leaving scarcely a trace behind him. Perhaps his capital fault was his separation from Wesley. He was certainly never designed by Providence to scatter so ineffectually his vast powers.

"Wesley was the counterpart of Whitefield. They were raised up to co-operate in one great cause—the one to construct its plans, the other to vivify them with the electric powers of his genius. The one held on his due course, and the results of his steadfastness are still developing on a scale of unparalleled grandeur. The other deviated; and almost the last vestige of his labors has passed away, or blended undistinguishably with the mass of the church.

"Like the great men of old, Wesley was careful in his physical habits. Though of a feeble constitution, his regularity, sustained through great exertions and vicissitudes, produced a vigor and equanimity which are seldom the accompaniments of a laborious mind or of a distracted life. He somewhere says he does not remember to have felt lowness of spirits one quarter of an hour since he was born—that ten thousand cares are no more weight to his mind than ten thousand hairs are to his head—and that he never lost a night's sleep in his life. Southey says, his face was remarkably fine, his complexion fresh to the last week of his life, and his eye quick, keen, and active.

"One of the finest spectacles to me is the sight of an old man holding on his career of action or endurance to the extremity of life with an unwavering spirit. Such was Wesley. He ceased not his labors till death. After the eightieth year of his age he visited Holland twice. At the end of his eighty-second, he says, 'I am never tired either with writing, preaching, or traveling.' He preached under trees which he had planted himself, at Kingswood. He outlived most of his first disciples and preachers, and stood up mighty in intellect and labors among the second and third generations of his people. I have been affected in reading the account of his later years, when persecution had subsided, and he was everywhere received as a patriarch, and sometimes, as his biographer says, he excited, by his arrival in towns and cities, an interest such as the king himself would produce. He attracted the largest assemblies, perhaps, which have been congregated for religious instruction since the ministry of Christ, being estimated sometimes at more than *thirty thousand*. Great intellectually, morally, and physically, he at length died, in the eighty-eighth year of his age, and sixty-fifth of his ministry, unquestionably one of the most extraordinary men of any age.

"He lived to see Methodism spread through Great Britain, America, and the West India Islands. Nearly one hundred and forty thousand members, upward of five hundred itinerant preachers, and more than one thousand local preachers, were connected with him when he died. And how have these multiplied since! The epitaph of Sir Christopher Wren, in St. Paul's Cathedral, the work of his own genius, is applicable to Wesley's memory in almost all the civilized world: '*Do you ask for his monument? Look around you.*'"

A VISION IN THE WILDERNESS.

"It seemed a dream, and yet 'twas not."

In my long journeys in the West, I used frequently to rest during the heat of the noon-day under the shade of a tree, fastening my horse to one of its branches by a long rope, which afforded him ample room for grazing. After a hearty meal, of the famed "*hoe-cake*," furnished at my last stopping place, and eaten with a relish which nothing but hunger and travel can give, and offering up my tribute of praise to Him who guided my wanderings, I usually lay down on my traveling blanket, with my saddle for a pillow, and refreshed myself by a few hours' sleep. Reposing thus, with my pocket Bible in my hand, reading and meditating on the promises of God to his people, I once fell into a dreamy revery, during which I imagined that all the illustrious of the church in former ages passed in slow procession before me.

First in the long train, and at considerable distance from the following groups, moved a venerable company, with silvered locks, and elevated and wrinkled brows; their countenances were marked with an expression of blended gravity and simplicity, their staves were crooks, and their whole appearance indicated the simple habits of pastoral life. They were preceded by a figure of peculiar dignity, the rapt thoughtfulness of whose countenance bespoke a high communion with the spiritual world—a friendship with the Deity.

At a short distance in their rear followed one whose whole bearing was that of a stern, yet dignified consciousness of power. He bore in one hand a rod, and in the other a scroll. His brow seemed like bronze, and was marked with the lines of most profound and somewhat awful thought. I gazed on this ancient-looking group until the shadows of the foremost grew dim in the distance, when, turning my eye, my attention was immediately arrested by an exceedingly interesting company of more varied character, and at more irregular intervals from each other. They were male and female. Their countenances wore different expressions; some the calm dignity of collected thought, others a lofty majesty that seemed something more than human; some an affecting pathos and lonely sadness, while the features of others were radiant with the outbreakings of ecstatic emotion. All, however, had an indefinable correspondence. I was struck with an uplifted look of the eyes that was common to all, and imparted an aspect of sanctified inspiration.

The first in the group was a lovely female figure, whose graceful form appeared to glide along as if moving on the air; her hair waved in the breezes, and her countenance was an expression of blended beauty and holiness. It seemed illuminated with a radiance from heaven. In one hand she held above her head a timbrel, while with the other she struck it with enthusiasm. At a distance methought I heard her sing, "Awake, awake, Deborah; awake, awake, utter a song."

Next followed an unimpassioned, aged man, his eyes sunken, and his locks white like the snows of winter; mature thought and wise counsel sat on his visage, blended with a hallowed complacency that seemed to say, "Speak, Lord, for thy servant heareth." He was followed by one who was robed in regal apparel, and whose head was circled with a crown. He appeared a prince of God's people, anointed from on high. His face shone with rapture as he moved buoyantly along, with a harp in his hand, singing "O come, let us sing unto the Lord;

let us make a joyful noise unto the Rock of our salvation."

Then came one wrapped in a mantle, with a solemnity truly august; his beard was long and silvery; his eye, though sunken with age, gleamed with fire; and on his elevated, bu indented brow, sat a solemn loftiness of thought. His motion was that of strong old age, and as he passed I heard him say, "Awake, awake; put on thy strength, O Zion; put on thy beautiful garments, O Jerusalem, the holy city."

In the same group I observed several other most interesting figures, some carrying harps, some rejoicing, some weeping. Among the latter, one particularly affected me. He seemed a man of God—his look was that of deep dejection, yet submissive and sanctified. He uttered as he passed, with a tone of affecting pathos, "O that my head were waters, and mine eyes a fountain of tears, that I might weep day and night for the slain of the daughter of my people!"

Many others of remarkable appearance were passing before me, but the sudden approach of another group at a distance drew away my attention. The first that caught my eye was a figure robed in camel's hair, with a leathern girdle about his loins; his face was weather-worn, as if he were accustomed to an exposed life. His gait was dignified and grave; his voice, owing to the distance, was very indistinct, but, associated with his whole personal appearance, it was as "the voice of one crying in the wilderness." Then followed one whose step was slow and godlike. A singular combination of power and goodness was expressed in all his bearing. At one moment I thought it might be an impersonated image of greatness and might—and at another, of meekness and lowliness. An indescribable benignity shone on his features, and yet a cloud of sorrow seemed to wreathe his brow, so that he appeared indeed " a man of sorrows, and acquainted with grief."

Then followed a company that could not so well be called a group as a file, owing to their great extent. The first seemed men of much simplicity of character, unpretending in their manners, but conscious of high powers and great responsibilities; a calm fearlessness was expressed in their countenances. Among them I observed two figures that particularly interested my attention; the first for his delightful complacency. His whole countenance beamed with amiable lowliness and compassion, and he appeared to be uttering to himself as he passed, "God is love." The other looked accustomed to the patient and wearying .oil of the laborious scholar. An expression of contemplative thoughtfulness was expanded over his brow. He appeared like one whose mind was pregnant with mighty thoughts, and who could stand unmoved in the integrity of his principles before the thrones of kings and amid the schools of philosophers. Though his countenance was that of a great man, yet it wore a holy humility that seemed to say, "God forbid that I should glory, save in the cross of our Lord Jesus Christ!" After the first few figures, the number increased rapidly, till it appeared like the hosts of war; their countenances bespoke heroic boldness and contempt of pain, as if they were familiar with perils and death—panoplied pilgrims, who have here no abiding place, but seek a city eternal in the heavens. After some hundreds had passed, the procession seemed to terminate, and dense darkness followed; dim, phantasmagoric figures, more like shapes of shadow than living beings, appeared for a moment, and then faded away in the gloom; but I continued to gaze anxiously for some new and more distinct appearance, when suddenly one emerged, wearing the cowl and girdle of a monk. In his hand he grasped a rusty parchment copy of the Bible. Defiance was written on his brow. His step was firm and determined, and, though clouds and darkness surrounded him, he daringly advanced, and they seemed to retire, while light broke out in his footsteps. The concourse that followed in his train became so numerous as to confuse my thoughts. Not being able to distinguish them minutely, I began to contemplate them in the gross—their vast extent—the new accessions continually rising up to my view. On looking upward, a sublime object riveted my attention. It was a cross of fire flaming out on a dark cloud, and above it was written, in letters of light, *Conquer by this*. The prospect was constantly opening and extending around. The clouds that circumscribed it at first were rolling further and further into the distance. I followed the multiplying host with my eye as they passed along, and observed at each movement in their progress the ruins of overturned altars, gory with recent sacrifices—temples tottering to the earth—fragments of thrones, commingled with broken fetters and sundered chains. The darkness became less and less, until, gathering itself into one mass, like a cloud highly surcharged with lightning, it passed away with a great noise, when the whole prospect assumed a thousand varied aspects of light and beauty. The host I was contemplating, now so numerous as to spread over the entire survey, cried aloud, "The kingdoms of this world have become the kingdoms of our Lord and of his Christ, and he shall reign for ever and ever," followed by a shout from heaven, saying, "Allelujah, for the Lord God omnipotent reigneth!" at which I awoke, and lo, it was a dream!

CHILDREN OF RELIGIOUS PARENTS.

"Train up a child in the way he SHOULD *go."*
Solomon.

My heart still bleeds when I recall the death-scene of my old friend W. He was a good man, and is no doubt at rest. He labored usefully as a local preacher, and scores were converted from the error of their ways by his instrumentality; but of all his numerous children, only one daughter, who ministered as an angel at his sick bed, had acknowledged the name of Christ. Two of his sons had died in responsible years, without hope, one of them in agonies of despair: the spirit of the old man never recovered from the shock. Three were still living; two, wandering he knew not where, the votaries of dissipation, the other confined in a neighboring alms-house, a maniac. Seldom have I known an equal case of domestic affliction. He had educated his family in religion with all diligence, but was now dying, with the hope of meeting but one of them in heaven. The affections of the parent were naturally strong in him, but in his last sickness they were overpowering. "Pray for my children," was his pathetic appeal to the Christian friends who visited him—" O my children! My poor boys! I go down to the grave in sorrow for them. Must they be lost? Cannot prayer still pluck them as brands from the burning? Pray, O pray for my children!" The Christian parent alone can feel the force of this dying father's language, and even he cannot feel as I do, while recalling the unutterable anxiety of his emaciated features, bathed as they were with the tears of paternal tenderness. Ah! it is on the margin of eternity—it is when the soul, full of unspeakable solicitude, feels that it is passing returnlessly away, that the affections receive a depth of pathos they never had before. It is then, too, that we see things as they are;—valuable only so far as they relate to the endless state into which we are passing

It is then, mistaken parent, that thou wilt wish to see thy child lying, with the hopes and woes of Lazarus, at the gate of the rich man, rather than enjoying, without God, the admiration or wealth for which thou art now so anxiously training it.

The old man expired, praying for his children, and his prayer was not altogether in vain; for " God is not slack concerning his promises; and he has assured the Christian parent that " it shall be well with him, and his children after him ;" that " the generation of the upright shall be blessed." His poor maniac son has since been restored, and is now seen " sitting at the feet of Jesus, clothed and in his right mind." His name is on the temperance pledge and the church book, and I trust it is " written in heaven." One of his brothers has also been reclaimed, and the other still lives, and is therefore within the reach of the many prayers which have ascended for him.

I have not introduced this case in order to sketch it, but to append a few thoughts on an important subject. It is an interesting question why the children of religious parents are so seldom converted, and not unfrequently are more hostile to religion than those who have had no early religious training. The reasons usually assigned are, that they become disgusted with religion by the importunity of their parents; that severe early restraints become irksome, and react; that the imperfections which they observe in the domestic conduct of their relatives destroy their confidence, &c., &c. I doubt most of the usual reasoning on this subject. It may apply in particular cases, but it does not solve the whole problem. Where these defects have not existed, the result has been the same. The most painful examples I have known were in the families of devoted and judicious ministers, some of whose children, whom I can at this moment recall, are reeling to the grave drunkards. I think the reason lies deeper than is usually conjectured. There is a profound fault somewhere in our system of religious training. The constitution of the human mind requires the Scriptural mode of enforcing religion, and admits of no other, and this is not the mode adopted in the religious education of children. Let me explain.

We have two classes of habits, passive and active. The facility of the former is diminished, while that of the latter is increased, by exercise. The surgeon, in the beginning of his profession, may feel a painful sympathy for the sufferings of his patient. This very sympathy may unnerve his hand, and embarrass his operation. By familiarity with suffering his sympathies harden—the *passive* susceptibility abates, until the agonies of his writhing subject scarcely discompose his feelings. But with this decrease of feeling there is an increase of tact in the use of his instruments—the *active* habit is improved, so that the most unfeeling operators are generally the most accurate and secure. The experience of the drunkard is another example; in proportion as he advances in his vicious habit does his susceptibility of agreeable excitement diminish. The draught that at first intoxicated becomes powerless, and, to have effect, must be increased as he advances.

This interesting law applies equally to our moral nature. Let an individual be passive, but inactive, amid the examples and admonitions of religion, and he will inevitably degenerate. So well known is this fact, that the popular language, without scrutinizing the reason, has characterized such as " gospel hardened." The most thrilling appeals of truth fall on their ears like the breath of the wind, while others, a hundred-fold more debased in vice, but less accustomed to religious motives, quake with trembling. Now, does not this consideration explain the irreligion of the children of religious

parents? They witness constantly examples of
religion, but is it the case that parents *labor
directly* for their conversion? It is to be feared
that *direct efforts* for the salvation of children
are rare. We teach them its doctrines, and
discipline them to some of its moralities, but do
we treat them as the *gospel treats sinners*—
urging them to immediate repentance and faith
as the means of regeneration and the ground of
all true practical virtue? I have often thought, in
my observations on Christian families, that the
indirectness with which religious impressions
were made was exactly adapted to habituate
the mind to easy resistance. Witnessing daily
the examples of religion without any active
participation in them, they are preparing either
to doubt and despise all religion, or hang on our
congregations lifeless moralists.

Our religious feelings must be active, or they
will decline. Like the vigor of the body, they
depend upon exercise. Nothing could more
effectually benumb the heart of a philanthropist,
than to observe daily the miseries of the suffering without an effort to relieve them.

Let not, then, the Christian parent try to in
troduce his child to religion by a gradual process
of discipline—this is good in its place—but let
him first teach and urge an immediate renewal

of the heart—the same as is necessary in an adult sinner, for sin is as radical in the nature of a child as in that of a man of threescore years and ten—and then, being introduced to the active habits of religion, both inward and outward, they will grow with its growth.

These thoughts suggest an admonition to the children of religious families. How great are their privileges! The light of heaven shines upon their infant brows in the very cradle. Their house is a miniature sanctuary, with its altar of morning and evening sacrifice. The oracles of truth speak to them daily with wiser counsels than angels could utter. The sweetest affections of life are made to them vehicles of religious influence. How can it be possible for a child to grow up in habitual resistance of all these appeals, and not suffer seriously in his moral susceptibility? His heart must become indurated. These blessings will be either a savor of life unto life, or of death unto death.

Child of many prayers! thou art blessed indeed; but O! be warned that thy mercies turn not to curses, and that the sweet memories of thy home be not imbittered through eternity

THE DUEL.

"Blood-guiltiness!"—Psalmist.

About four miles from N—— is an extensive grove, well known as the scene of several fatal duels. As I passed it one morning on my way to my appointment in that town, I perceived a horse and vehicle among the trees, guarded by a solitary man, who appeared to be the driver. My suspicions were immediately aroused, but I rode on.

About a mile beyond I met another carriage, containing four persons, besides the driver, and hastening with all speed. My fears were confirmed, and I could scarcely doubt that another scene of blood was about to be enacted in those quiet solitudes. What was my duty in the case? I knew too well the tenacity of those fictitious and absurd sentiments of honor which prevailed in that section of the country, and which gave to the duel a character of exalted chivalry, to hope that my interference could be successful; yet, thought I, it is my duty to rebuke the sin, if I cannot prevent it, and in the name of my Lord I will do it. As quick as the thought, I wheeled about, and returned with the utmost speed to the grove.

The second carriage had arrived, and was fastened to a tree. I rode up to it, fastened my horse near it, and throwing the driver a piece of silver, requested him to guard him. While threading my way into the forest, my thoughts were intensely agitated to know how to present myself most successfully. The occasion admitted of no delay. I hastened on, and soon emerged into an oval space surrounded on all sides by the dense woods. At the opposite extremities stood the principals, their boots drawn over their pantaloons, their coats, vests, and hats off, and with handkerchiefs tied over their heads, and tightly belting their waists. A friend and a surgeon were conversing with each, while the seconds were about midway between them, arranging the dreadful conflict. One of the principals, the challenged, appeared but about twenty years old; his countenance was singularly expressive of sensibility, but also of cool determination. The other had a stout, ruffian-like bearing, a countenance easy, but sinister and heartless, and seemed impatient to wreak his vengeance on his antagonist.

I advanced immediately to the seconds, and declared at once my character and my object. "Gentlemen," said I, "excuse my intrusion; I am a minister of the gospel; I know not the merits of this quarrel, but both my heart and my office require me to mediate a peace between the parties, if possible. Is it not possible?"

"Sir," replied one of them, "the utmost has been done to effect it, without success, and this is no place for further attempts."

"Under any circumstances, in any place, gentlemen," I replied, "it is appropriate to prevent murder, and such, in the sight of God, is the deed you are aiding. It must not be, gentlemen: in the name of the law, which prohibits it—in the name of your friends, the principals—in the name of God, who looks upon you in this solitary place, I beseech you, stop it at once; at least, wash your own hands from the blood of these men; retire from the field, and refuse to assist in their mutual murder."

My emphatic remonstrance had a momentary effect; they seemed not indisposed to come to terms, if I could get the concurrence of the principals.

I passed immediately to the oldest of them His countenance became more repulsive as I approached him; it was deeply pitted with the small-pox, and there was upon it the most Satanic, cold-blooded leer I ever witnessed on a human face. He had given the challenge. I besought him, by every consideration of humanity and morality, to recall it. I referred to the youth and inexperience of his antagonist, the conciliatory disposition of the seconds, the fearful consequences to his soul if he should fall, the withering remorse which must ever follow him if he should succeed.

He evidently thirsted for the blood of his opponent; but observing that his friend and the surgeon seconded my reasoning, he replied, with undissembled reluctance, that he gave the challenge for sufficient reasons; if they were removed, he might recall it, but never otherwise.

I passed to the other. I admonished him of the sin he was about to perpetrate, and referred to his probable domestic relations. The allusion touched his heart; he suddenly wiped a tear from his eye. "Yes, sir," said he, "there are hearts which would break if they knew I were here." I referred to my conversation with the seconds and the other principal, and remarked that nothing was now necessary to effect a reconciliation but his retraction of the language which had offended his adversary. "Sir," he replied, planting his foot firmly on the earth, and assuming a look which would have been sublime in a better cause—" Sir, I have but declared the truth respecting that man, and though I sink into the grave, I will not sanction his villainous character by a retraction." I reasoned with increased vehemence, but no appeal to his judgment or his heart could shake his desperate firmness. My heart bled over this young man, and I left him with tears, which I have no doubt he would have shared under other circumstances. What could I do further? I appealed again to the principal, but he spurned me with a cool smile; I flew to the seconds, and requested them on any terms to adjust the matter and save the shedding of blood. But they had already measured the ground, and were ready to arrange the principals. "Gentlemen," said I, "the blood of this dreadful deed be upon your souls; I have acquitted myself of it;" and I proceeded from the arena toward my horse.

What were my emotions as I turned away in despair! What! thought I; must it proceed? Is there no expedient to prevent it? In a few minutes one or both of these men may be in eternity, accursed for ever with "blood guiltiness!" Can I not pluck them as brands from the burning? My spirit was in a tumult of anxiety. In a moment, as the principals were taking their places, I was again on the ground, standing on the line between them. "Sirs!"

I exclaimed, " in the name of God, I adjure you stop this murderous work. It must not, it cannot proceed."

" Knock him down," cried the elder duelist, with a fearful imprecation.

" Sir," said the younger, " I appreciate your motives, but demand of you to interfere no more with these arrangements."

The seconds seized me by the arm, and compelled me to retire. But I warned them at every step. Never before did I feel so deeply the value and hazard of the human soul. My remarks were without effect, except on one of the friends of the younger principal. " This is a horrible place," said he ; " I cannot endure it;" and he turned away with me from the scene.

" Now, then, for it," said one of the seconds, as they returned ; " take your places." Shudderingly I hastened my pace to escape the result.

" One, two "—the next sound was lost in the explosion of the pistols. " O God !" shrieked a voice of agony. I turned round ; the younger principal, with his hand to his face, shrieked again, quivered, and fell to the earth. I rushed to him. With one hand he clung to the earth, the fingers penetrating the sod, with the other he grasped his left jaw, which was shattered with a horrid wound. I turned with faintness from the sight. The charge had passed through the left side of the mouth, crashing the teeth, severing the jugular, and passing out at the back of the head, laying open entirely one side of the face and neck. In this ghastly wound, amid blood and shattered teeth, had he fixed his grasp with a tenacity which could not be moved. Bleeding profusely, and convulsive with agony, he lay for several minutes, the most frightful spectacle I had ever witnessed. The countenances of the spectators expressed a conscious relief when it was announced by the surgeon that death had ended his agony. Meanwhile the murderer, with his party, had left the ground.

One of the company was dispatched, on my horse, to communicate the dreadful news to the family of the victim. The dead young man was cleansed from his blood, and borne immediately to the carriage. I accompanied it into N——. It stopped before a small, but elegant house. The driver ran to the door and rapped An elderly lady opened it with frantic agitation, at the instant when we were lifting the ghastly remains from the carriage. She gazed, as if thunderstruck, for a moment, and fell fainting in the doorway. A servant removed her into the parlor, and as we passed with the corpse into a rear room, I observed her extended on a sofa as pale as her hapless son. We had just laid the body on a table—the stiffened hand still grasping the wound—when a young lady, tastefully attired in white, and with a face delicately beautiful, rushed into the room and threw her arms around it, weeping with uncontrollable emotion, and exclaiming with agony of feeling, "My brother!—my dear, dear brother!—Can it be—O, can it be?" The attendants tore her away. I shall never forget the look of utter wretchedness she wore as they led her past me, her eyes suffused with tears, and her bosom stained with her brother's blood.

This unfortunate young man was of New-England origin. He had settled in the town of N——, where his business prospered so well that he had invited his mother and sister to reside with him. His home, endeared by gentleness and love, and every temporal comfort, was a scene of unalloyed happiness; but in an evil hour he yielded to a local and absurd prejudice, a sentiment of honor, falsely so called, which his education should have taught him to despise. He was less excusable than his malicious murderer, for he had more light and better sentiments. This one step ruined him and his happy family. He was interred the next day, with the regrets of the whole community. His poor mother never left the house till she was carried to her grave, by his side. She died after a delirious fever of two weeks' duration throughout which she ceased not to implore the attendants, with tears, to rescue her hapless son from the hands of assassins, who she imagined kept him concealed for their murderous purpose. His sister still lives, but poor and broken-hearted. Her beauty and her energies, nave been wasted by sorrow, and she is dependent on others for her daily bread.

I have heard some uncertain reports of his antagonist; the most probable of which is, that he died three years after of the yellow fever at New-Orleans, raging with the horrors of remorse. Such was the local estimation of this bloody deed, that scarcely an effort was made to bring him to justice. Alas, for the influence of fashionable opinion! It can silence, by its dictates, the laws of man and of God, and exalt murder to the glory of chivalry.

BISHOP ASBURY.

" A workman that needeth not to be ashamed.'
St. Paul.

To have enjoyed the friendship of the great and good Asbury may well be considered a distinguished honor—his autographs on the ordination certificates of the fathers of the church are precious mementoes, and more satisfactory authentications of their ministry than could be the sign manual of any pope, archbishop, or other supposed successor of the apostles. If there are any episcopal seats in heaven, assuredly there are few prelates since St. Paul who will sit above Francis Asbury.

His marked characteristics are few, but remarkably strong. They are not painted, in our conception of his character, but sculptured. He was altogether a most wonderful man. Born in lowly circumstances, called early to the ministry, and when in it burdened with labors truly amazing, he had but little opportunity for mental cultivation. Yet he acquired (how, is inconceivable) a knowledge of Latin, Greek, and Hebrew; he could read them, and consulted them in studying the sacred text. He was also singularly familiar with history.

especially ecclesiastical history. Church polity, in all its varieties, ancient and modern, he had studied thoroughly, and referred to constantly. In mental and moral science he was more than a mere reader. In natural philosophy he was generally accurate. He was a more extensive reader than is generally supposed. He had no knowledge of mathematics, and his arithmetic was altogether original—logical, not mechanical. He possessed an almost intuitive discernment of human character, and was a remarkable physiognomist. He had frequently surprised a whole conference by stating the character of candidates whom he had never seen before. He had a rare facility in contracting the acquaintance of strangers. He was frequently humorous, happy at repartee, and always ready for any labor, however onerous or sudden. An illustration occurs to my memory. At the time my friend E. H. was stationed in B———, knowing that he would spend a night there on his way to the L——— Conference, he made arrangements for him to preach an anniversary sermon for a charitable society just struggling into life, and advertised the appointment as extensively as possible in the public prints. Toward evening the old bishop arrived, wearied with a long and tedious journey. At an early hour the house was crowded —the services commenced. He arose, and read for his text 2 Corinthians viii, 8, "I speak not by commandment, but by occasion of the forwardness of others, and to prove the sincerity of your love." The felicity of the text and of the discourse was universally observed.

If the classical motto is true, *Perseverantia vincit omnià*, (Perseverance conquers all things,) he was capable of greatness in any department of human ambition, for his great master trait was a firmness of purpose which no hostility could shake and no allurement seduce. When once he entered on his immense labors in America, his destiny was fixed. His indomitable energy bore him onward through journeys long and perilous, labors arduous and incessant, privations and vexations which none of his European coadjutors knew, and this, not during a brief interval of youthful zeal, or of circumstances auspicious to an ardent ambition, but through all possible discouragements, and through the infirmities of age, when it was necessary to assist him to and from his carriage, and when he could no longer stand, but sat in the pulpit,—till, in fine, he dropped exhausted into the grave. He was eminently a man of one work, and in that work he was impelled by a quenchless zeal, which allowed no leisure for any other consideration. It drew him away from his native land and parental home, and permitted no return. It induced him to forego the felicities of domestic life, and to pass through a long career without a local habitation or a resting place. He was a noble example of an evangelical bishop. He possessed all the personal dignity of the episcopal office, without any of the assumed honors and luxurious exemptions which are usually connected with it. While he directed with inflexible authority the ministerial host of his vast diocese, he transcended the meanest of them in sufferings, labors, and journeyings. Fifty-five years he was a preacher, and forty-five of them he spent on our continent. It has been estimated that he sat in two hundred and twenty-four annual conferences, and consecrated about four thousand ministers.

I have said that his labors and sufferings were unequaled by those of his transatlantic coadjutors. He traveled usually about six thousand miles a year, which exceeded the journeyings of Wesley. Wesley's field was much less extended, and much more comfortable in every respect. He was in his own country—had the best facilities for traveling—

and moved through a nation supplied with all the conveniences of life. Asbury was a foreigner, and lived among us at a period of profound antipathy toward his native land; but when most others fled from the field he remained, even though concealment was necessary. The country was new and vast, yet he traveled over its length and breadth, now through its older settlements, and then along its frontier lines, climbing mountains, fording streams, sleeping under the trees of the forest, or finding shelter for his wearied frame in log cabins.

Whitefield, though he traveled over the same continent, confined himself to its Atlantic cities, where every convenience was lavishly afforded him. Asbury pushed his course to the remotest frontier, traveling frequently with the emigrating caravan for protection from the savage, and thanking God for the coarse fare which was afforded him in the hut of the back-woodsman. Whitefield's theological opinions agreed with the errors of the dominant churches, and conciliated their favor. Asbury's were detested by them as among the worst forms of heresy. Methodism had commenced before nis arrival on our continent, and no doubt would have prospered more or less, but to his energy must be ascribed its wonderful progress. Spread by his exertions, no barrier could stand before it; it broke out on the right and on the left; his incessant preaching and ceaseless traveling, now in the north and then in the south, now in the east and then in the west, gave it almost an omnipresent and simultaneous action through all the states. Though at the commencement of his labors in this country there were *but six hundred* members in the church, when he fell it was victoriously at the head of *an army of two hundred and twelve thousand*, who were still exulting in their strength, and pressing on to the spiritual conquest of the land, like the hosts of war to the charge!

Wonderful man! many of similar, but none of equal powers, have followed in his footsteps. With a ministry of such spirits, the regeneration of our race would be the achievement of a single age. Such a ministry, warring with the mighty agencies of evil in our world, would present the sublime spectacle of Milton's battle of the angels. And such a ministry (soul-stirring thought!) is practicable. It was not the possession of those powers which form the prerogatives of genius that made Asbury what he was. He displayed no splendid endowments of intellect. His greatness arose more from *dispositions* than from *talents*. Zeal, love of man, and love of God, armed him with his power, and these are attainable by all. They gave him that determination of purpose which bore down all that opposed it, and made him "mighty through God," equaling in labors and success Whitefield, or even Wesley, without the genius of the one or the learning of the other. While most of the great men who guided the early movements of Methodism are illustrations of the power of sanctified intellect, Asbury seems to have been providentially raised up and placed among them as an example of the power of the ordinary faculties of man when sustained by high moral motives, a sublime model, not for the talented, like the former, *but for all.* It has been justly remarked that he occupies the place in the religious history of this country which Washington does in its civil history Methodism, toward which, on this continent, he sustained the relation of leader, has already outstripped all other sects, but is still in its childhood: all its operations are yet in their incipience. What will be its importance when it reaches maturity? Then, perhaps, the honor we claim for Asbury will be conceded. Methodism, under Asbury, gave the impulse which roused most other sects, and spread over the country the spirit of revivals. The time will yet come when he will be acknowledged, not merely the father of American Methodism, but of *American evangelism.*

PRESENTIMENTS.

"Secret things belong unto the Lord our God."
Moses.

I HAVE lately received the Life of Mr. Watson. The biographer, in relating his visit with Watson to a certain village, says, " In passing the church-yard, Mr. Watson pointed to a conspicuous grave, and said, ' The first time I traveled this way, that grave-stone caught my eye, especially the words * * *, who died, aged forty-two. A very strong impression, for which I could not account, was immediately made upon my mind, that I should die at precisely the same age. The impression was both strong and sudden; I have already passed that age, and this shows how little stress can be justly laid upon those sudden impulses and impressions, of which some people make so much account.' This impression, it appears, had created considerable uneasiness in the family of Mr. Watson ; but its effect on his own mind it is not easy to determine."

Watson possessed a vigorous mind, one that we should suppose would be the last to indulge fanatical or whimsical ideas ; we may learn, therefore, from his case, the liability of weaker minds to be deluded by such impressions. Had he been as susceptible as his anxious family, it is not improbable that he would have worn away under the impression, fallen into some fatal disease, and expired at the precise time, and all this the result merely of imagination. Medical history is full of proofs on this subject, and it is altogether probable that most who die under such circumstances fall victims to their own folly, instead of a revealed design of Providence. Cases have been known where criminals condemned to death have been blindfolded, laid upon the block, slightly struck on the neck with a cane, and taken up dead, without the loss of a drop of blood.

It is singular with what tenacity these morbid fears will cling to the mind, especially when the system has been enervated by prolonged excitement. No class of men, perhaps, are more exposed to such excitement than Methodist preachers, by both their extemporaneous mode of speaking, which is accompanied often with intense emotion, and the frequency and arduousness of their pastoral labors and social meetings; and perhaps most of them experience, at some time or other, its depressing effects.

My old friend M., when stationed at B——, had a brief and ludicrous attack of this species of hypochondria. He had labored arduously during several weeks, and not a few vexatious difficulties had disturbed the church and harassed his mind. On returning late, and quite exhausted, one night, from a meeting at which he had felt uncommonly languid and dejected, he was suddenly seized, as he entered his study, with the impression that he had offended God, and would die that very night. As usual with a diseased state of the mind, the thought was attended with profound melancholy. Of course he thought not of sleep, but walked the floor in agony for hours. Wearied at last by his rapid paces, he seated himself, and, covering his face with his hands, reclined his head on a table. Thus situated, he prayed, wept, and trembled, and as the time advanced, prayed, wept, and trembled the more. At last, in his agony, and with his hair on end, he rose to pace again the floor, when, lo! daylight was streaming in at his window! The illusion was gone, and the astonished man knew not whether he ought to smile or blush at his weakness. It was a weakness, however, which a superior mind can more easily despise than prevent.

It was my own misfortune once to suffer much from one of these presentiments of death. It was received while I was upon my knees in private prayer. The circumstances were strong, the impression at the time was singularly clear and forcible, like an intuition. Subsequent circumstances, too, seemed confirmatory of it. The very next day an excellent Christian died in the neighborhood, who had entertained such a presentiment for months, and had even provided his coffin for the event. As the time passed the omens became stronger; by an accidental exposure I took cold, was attacked with cough, and confined to my room with incipient symptoms of pulmonary consumption. How easily would some minds have given way under these circumstances, and have realized the expected result! I had not, however, been disposed to superstitious fears, and knew the caprices of the imagination, and its dangerous influence on health. I therefore calmly endeavored to prepare my mind and circumstances for any result, and waited through the period of several weeks, within which I expected to die,

and which terminated precisely with the year.
During this time I was confined to my room;
the impression was inseparably present; I
treated it with respect, but not with fear—it
might be from God, or it might not. The last
night came, but still there were a few hours,
and what might not occur in them! I watched
until midnight, and not until the clock announced
that the last moment of the year had flown was
I clear from this remarkable illusion. I then
fell upon my knees, thanked God that I had
not fallen a victim to this weakness, and prayed
that I might better remember that "the secret
things belong to the Lord our God; but those
things which are revealed belong unto us, and
to our children for ever, that we may do all
the words of his law." It cannot be said that
God does not, in rare instances, reveal their
dying hours to his people; but I never knew a
case which could be relied on, and the best
reasons apply against such a course on the part
of his providence.

ANECDOTES OF JESSE LEE.

"A soft answer turneth away wrath."—Solomon.

Jesse Lee was a genuine specimen of the first school of Methodist preachers. Like Asbury, he remained unmarried, that he might give himself wholly to the ministry of the word. Asbury prized him highly, and without doubt wished his appointment as his own coadjutor or successor, showing his confidence in his abilities for the office, by using him as his substitute in attending annual conferences and appointing the preachers. In labors he was abundant, and many of the churches, from Maine to Georgia, still preserve recollections of him. His eloquence was sometimes remarkable, smiting the conscience with remorse, or melting the heart with uncontrollable emotion. His person was large, and his countenance at once expressive of two traits, which, though somewhat opposite, were nevertheless united and predominant in his nature—tenderness and shrewdness. Though he could weep with those who wept, few men have been happier at repartee. Satire is a dangerous weapon, and perhaps it was his fault, but he often used it with the best effect. Many a conceited gainsayer, in attempting, after his sermons' in the open air, to embarrass him on metaphysical points, has cowered beneath his replies, and retreated in mortification and wonder. My lamented old friend, Dr. Thomas Sargent, (himself one of the pioneers,) has assured me that the current anecdote of the Methodist preacher's reply to two lawyers on extemporary preaching actually occurred with Jesse Lee. The shrewd itinerant had been preaching in a town during the session of the court, and had dealt rather faithfully with the lawyers, two of whom were disposed to make themselves merry at his expense. The day on which the court adjourned he left the place for another appointment. While riding on his way, he perceived the two lawyers hastening after him on horseback, with evident expectations of amusement. They entered into conversation with him on extemporaneous speaking. "Don't you often make mistakes?" said one of them. "Yes, sir." "Well, what do you do with them?—Let them go?" "Sometimes I do," replied the preacher, drily; "if they are very important, I correct them; if not, or if they express the truth, though differently from what I designed, why, I often let them go. For instance, if, in preaching, I should wish to quote the text which says, 'The devil is a liar, and the father of it,' and should happen to misquote it, and say he was a '*lawyer,*' &c., why, it is so near the truth, I should probably let it pass." The gentlemen of the bar looked at each other, and were soon in advance, hastening on their way.

Many anecdotes are still related among the old Methodists who knew him, which illustrate his Christian meekness. The following is one. I am indebted for it to his nephew, Rev. L. M. Lee, who says the anecdote may be relied on as having really transpired. It was communicated to a member of the family under the following circumstances, by the individual most involved in the affair:—Some few years since a nephew of Mr. Lee, engaged in some business transaction in a store in Petersburg, Virginia, and being addressed as Mr. Lee, attracted the attention of an aged gentleman, General P., at the same time in the store, who immediately accosted him, and asked if he was a kinsman of the Rev. Jesse Lee. On being informed that he was a nephew, the general said he had long desired to see some member of the old minister's family, in order to communicate a circumstance that once occurred between himself and Mr. Lee. On being told that it would afford him pleasure to hear anything concerning his venerable relative, the general proceeded to relate in substance the following narrative:—

"When I was a young man, I went to hear Mr. Lee preach at —— meeting-house. There was a very large crowd in attendance, and a great many could not get into the house. Among others I got near the door, and being fond of show and frolic, I indulged in some indiscretion, for which Mr. Lee mildly, but plainly reproved me. In an instant all the bad feelings of my heart were roused. I was deeply insulted, and felt that my whole family was disgraced. I retired from the crowd to brood over the insult, and meditate revenge. It was not long before I resolved to whip him before he left the ground. I kept the resolution to myself; and watched, with the eager intensity of resentment, the opportunity to put it in execution. But the congregation was dismissed and dispersed, and I saw nothing of the preacher. How he escaped me I could never learn. I looked on every hand, scrutinized every departing group, but saw nothing of the man I felt I hated, and was resolved to whip. I went home sullen, mortified, and filled with revenge. My victim had escaped me. But I 'nursed my wrath to keep it warm;' and cherished the determination to put it into execution the first time I saw Mr. Lee, although long years should intervene. Gradually, however, my feelings subsided, and my impressions of the insult became weaker and less vivid; and in the lapse of a few years the whole affair faded away from my mind. Thirteen years passed over me, and the impetuosity of youth had been softened down by sober manhood, and gradually-approaching age I was standing upon 'the downhill of life.' On a beautiful morning in the early spring, I left my residence to transact some business in Petersburg; and on reaching the main road leading to town, I saw, a few hundred yards before me, an elderly-looking man jogging slowly along in a single gig. As soon as I saw him, it struck me, That's Jesse Lee. The name, the man, the sight of him recalled all my recollections of the insult, and all my purposes of resentment. I strove to banish them all from my mind. I reasoned on the long years that had intervened since the occurrence; the impropriety of thinking of revenge, and the folly of executing a purpose formed in anger, and after so long a lapse of time. But the more I thought, the warmer I became. My resolution stared me in the face; and something whispered coward in my heart if I failed to fulfill it. My mind was in a perfect tumult, and my passions waxed strong. I determined to execute my resolution to the utmost; and full of rage I spurred my horse, and was soon at the side of the man that I felt of all others I hated most.

"I accosted him rather rudely with the question, 'Are you not a Methodist preacher?'

"'I pass for one,' was the reply, and in a manner that struck me as very meek.

"'An't your name Jesse Lee?'

"'Yes: that's my name.'

"'Do you recollect preaching in the year —— at —— meeting-house?'

"'Yes; very well.'

"'Well, do you recollect reproving a young man on that occasion for some misbehavior?'

"After a short pause for recollection, he replied, 'I do.'

"'Well,' said I, 'I am that young man; and I determined that I would whip you for it the first time I saw you. I have never seen you from that day until this; and now I intend to execute my resolution and whip you.'

"As soon as I finished speaking, the old man stopped his horse, and looking me full in the face, said, 'You are a younger man than I am. You are strong and active; and I am old and feeble. I have no doubt but, if I were disposed to fight, you could whip me very easily; and it would be useless for me to resist. But as a "man of God, I must not strive." So as you are determined to whip me, if you will just wait, I will get out of my gig, and get down on my knees, and you may whip me as long as you please.'

"Never," said the old general, "was I so suddenly and powerfully affected. I was completely overcome. I trembled from head to foot. I would have given my estate if I had never mentioned the subject. A strange weakness came over my frame. I felt sick at heart; ashamed, mortified, and degraded, I struck my spurs into my horse, and dashed along the road with the speed of a madman. What became of the good old man I know not. I never saw him after that painfully-remembered morning. He has long since passed away from the earth; and has reaped the reward of the good, the gentle, and the useful, in a world where 'the wicked cease from troubling, and the weary find eternal rest.'

"I am now old; few and full of evil have been the days of the years of my life, yet I am not now without hope in God. I have made my peace with him who is 'the Judge of the quick and dead;' and hope ere long to see that good man of God with feelings very different from those with which I met him last."

The old man ceased. A glow of satisfaction spread over his features, and a tear stood in his eye. He seemed as if a burden was removed from his heart—that he had disencumbered himself of a load that had long pressed upon his spirits. He had given his secret to the near relative of the man he had once intended to injure, but whose memory he now cherished with feelings akin to those that unite the redeemed to each other, and bind the whole to "the Father of the spirits of all flesh."

THE MORAL SUBLIME.

" The sublime is an outward reflection of the inward greatness of the soul."—Longinus.

THE moral sublime is the sublime in moral action or endurance—the highest appeal to human taste. In an extensive review of ecclesiastical history which I have lately completed, I have been struck with the numerous examples which it affords of this noble greatness.

Profane history affords many sublime examples of endurance and self-sacrifice. The cases of Socrates, Leonidas, Regulus, and Winkelried, sustain our confidence in humanity and our hopes of the world. But how far short of the illustrious examples of the church are these instances! There is a peculiarity in the latter, arising from religious influence, which approaches the sublimity of inspiration. How calmly and majestically they suffer! What a bearing of repose, like the classic statues of the gods, they wear at the very stake, as if they were beings of a superior essence, immortal, and insensible to the effects of the elements! The instances of profane history are cases of cool and stanch submission to stern principle or hard necessity—magnanimous, indeed, but it is a dread magnanimity—a submission to suffering that is felt and endured, but not defied and vanquished. Those of religion are examples of calm triumph—of majestic superiority to suffering, as if they were conscious of being " more than conquerors." The former had fortitude, but the latter courage.

What an impressive specimen of the moral sublime is the last prayer of the gray-headed Polycarp, at the stake! He was nearly ninety years old; the veneration and affections of all the Asiatic churches centred in him. After being exposed to the hootings of the populace, and the aggravations of a mock trial, he was led to the place of death, where, being bound and all things ready for the match, he uttered this memorable prayer, or rather thanksgiving:—
" Father of thy well-beloved and blessed Son Jesus Christ, through whom we have received the knowledge of thee—God of angels and powers, and all creation, and of all the family of the righteous that live before thee—I bless thee that thou hast counted me worthy of this day, and of this hour,—an hour in which I am to have a share in the number of the martyrs and in the cup of Christ, unto the resurrection of eternal life, both of the soul and the body, in the incorruptible felicity of the Holy Spirit

Among whom may I be received this day, as a rich and acceptable sacrifice, which thou, the faithful and true God, hast prepared. Wherefore on this account and for all things I praise thee, I bless thee, I glorify thee, through the eternal High Priest, Jesus Christ, thy well-beloved Son. Through whom all glory be to thee with him in the Holy Ghost, both now and for ever. Amen." The flames curled over him and he was no more.

I scarcely know of a more sublime picture, though not an instance of violent suffering, than that of the death of the VENERABLE BEDE, as described by one of his pupils. He was the ornament of his country and of the eighth century, and was employed at the time of his death in rendering the Gospel of St. John into the language of the people, the Anglo-Saxon. " Many nights," says his disciple, " he passed without sleep, yet rejoicing and giving thanks, unless when a little slumber intervened. When he awoke he resumed his accustomed devotions, and with expanded hands never ceased giving thanks to God. By turns we read, and by turns we wept; indeed, we always read in tears. In such solemn joy we passed fifty days; but during these days, besides the lectures he gave, he endeavored to compose two works, one of which was a translation of St John into English. It has been observed of him, that he never knew what it was to do nothing. And after his breathing became still shorter, he dictated cheerfully, and sometimes said, '*Make haste;* I know not how long I shall hold out; my Maker may take me away very soon.' On one occasion, a pupil said to him, ' Most dear master, there is yet one chapter wanting; do you think it troublesome to be asked any more questions?' He answered, ' It is no trouble; take your pen and write *fast.*' He continued to converse cheerfully, and while his friends wept as he told them they would see him no more, they rejoiced to hear him say, ' It is now time for me to return to Him who made me. The time of my dissolution draws near. I desire to be dissolved and to be with Christ. Yes, my soul desires to see Christ in his beauty.' The pupil before mentioned said to him, ' Dear master, *one* sentence is still wanting.' He replied, ' *Write quickly.*' The young man soon added, ' It is finished.' He answered, ' Thou hast well said, all is now finished! Hold my head with thy hands. I shall delight to sit on the opposite side of the room, on the holy spot at which I have been accustomed to pray, and where, while sitting,

I can invoke my Father.' Being placed on the floor of his little room, he sung, ' Glory be to the Father, and to the Son, and to the Holy Ghost,' and died as he uttered the last word." What a scene for the painter! And one has painted it, not in colors, but in equally-expressive words : —

> —— Within his studious cell,
>   The man of mighty mind,
> His cowl'd and venerable brow
>   With sickness pale, reclined.
>
> " Speed on!" Then flew the writer's pen,
>   With grief and fear perplex'd;
> For death's sure footstep nearer drew
>   With each receding text.
> The prompting breath more faintly came—
>   " Speed on!—his form I see—
> That awful messenger of God,
>   Who may not stay for me."
>
> " *Master, 'tis done.*" " Thou speakest well
>   Life with thy lines kept pace."—
> They bear him to the place of prayer,
>   The death dew on his face;
> And there, while o'er the gasping breast
>   The last keen torture stole,
> With the high watchword of the skies,
>   Went forth that sainted soul.

THE CONVERTED DUTCHMAN.

"Now therefore ye are no more strangers and foreigners."—Paul.

Among my old ministerial acquaintances is the quaint B. H., now, like myself, on the "sick list" of the itinerant host. He was a pioneer evangelist among the Dutch settlers of New-York, and many are the humorous anecdotes which he gathered among those untutored, but honest-hearted rustics. He had a strong susceptibility of the humorous, and would often relate his comico-serious reminiscences with such effect as to excite one part of the company to tears and another to laughter, according to the serious or mirthful propensity of the hearer. One of these anecdotes I shall never forget. It was his favorite, and by repeated requests he was induced to put it on paper. I give it in his own words, for the words are essential to the sketch. It is the experience of a converted Dutchman, as stated by himself in a class meeting, and has always struck me as a correct representation of the workings of the human heart, and of the triumphs of grace over the stinted views of avarice. He said,—

"Mine dear bredren, I want to tell you some

mine experience. When de Metodists first came into dese parts, I tot I was doing bery well · for mine wife and I had two sons, Ned and Jim; and we had a good farm dat Neddy and I could work bery well, so I let Jim go out to work about fourteen miles off from home. But de Metodists come into our parts, and Neddy went to dare meeting, and he got converted, and I tot we should be all undone; so I told Ned he must not go to dese Metodists meetings, for so much praying and so much going to meeting would ruin us all. But Neddy said, 'O fader, I must serve de Lord and save my soul.' But, I said, you must do de work too. So I gave him a hard stint on de day of dere meeting; but he work so hard dat he got his stint done, and went to de meeting after all. While I set on mine stoop and smoked mine pipe, I see him go over de hill to de Metodist meeting, and I said to my wife, Elizabet, we shall be undone, for our Ned will go to dese meetings; and she said, 'What can we do?' Well, I said, den I will stint him harder; and so I did several times when de meeting come. But Neddy worked hard, and sometimes he got some boys to help him, so dat he would go off to de meeting while I set on mine stoop and smoked mine pipe. I could see Ned go over

de hill. I said one day, O mine Got, what can
I do—dis boy will go to dese meetings, after
all I can do! So when Ned come home I
said, Ned, you must leave off going to dese
meetings, or I will send for Jim to come home
and turn you away. But Neddy said, 'O fader.
I must serve de Lord and save my soul.' Well,
den, I will send for Jim: so I sent for Jim;
and when he come home, den I heard he had
been to de Metodist meeting where he had lived,
and he was converted too. And Ned and Jim
both said, 'O fader, we must serve de Lord and
save our souls.' But I said to mine wife, Dese
Metodists must be wrong; da will undo us all,
for da have got Ned and Jim both; I wish you
would go to dare meeting, and you can see
what is wrong; but Ned and Jim can't see it.
So de next meeting day de old woman went
wid Ned and Jim; but I set on mine stoop, and
smoked mine pipe. But I said to mine self, I
guess dese Metodists have got dar match to git
de old woman, and she will see what's wrong
So I smoked mine pipe, and looked to see dem
come back. By and by I see dem coming; and
when da come near I see de tears run down
mine wife's face. Den I said, O mine Got, da
have got de old woman too. I tot I am undone; for da have got Ned, and Jim, and de

old woman. And when da come on de stoop mine wife said, 'O we must not speak against dis people, for da are de people of Got.' But I said noting, for I had not been to any of de meetings, so I was in great trouble. But in a few days after I heard dat dare was a Presbyterian missionary going to preach a little ways off; so I tot I would go, for I tot it would not hurt anybody to go to his meeting; and I went wid Ned, and Jim, and mine wife, and he preached; but dere was noting done till after de meeting was over, and den dere was two young men in de toder room dat sung and prayed so good as anybody; and da prayed for dar old fader too. And many cried, and I tot da prayed bery well. After dis I was going out of de door to go home, and a woman said to me, 'Mr. ——, you must be a happy man to have two such young men as dem dat prayed.' I said, Was that Ned and Jim? She said, 'Yes.' O, I felt so mad to tink da had prayed for me, and exposed me before all de people. But I said noting, but went home, and I went right to bed. But now my mind was more troubled dan ever before, for I began to tink how wicked I was to stint poor Neddy so hard, and try to hinder him from saving his soul—but I said noting, and mine wife said noting; so I tried to go to sleep; but as soon as I shut mine eyes I could see Neddy going over de hill to go to his meeting, after he had done his hard stint, so tired and weary. Den I felt worse and worse; and by and by I groaned out, and mine wife axt me 'what's de matter?' I said, I believe I am dying. She said, 'Shall I call up Ned and Jim?' I said, Yes. And Jim come to de bed and said, 'O, fader, what is de matter?' I said, I believe I am dying. And he said, 'Fader, shall I pray for you?' I said, O yes, and Neddy too. And glory be to God, I believe he heard prayer; for tough I felt mine sins like a mountain load to sink me down to hell, I cried, O Got, have mercy on me, a poor sinner; and by and by I feel something run all over me, and split mine heart all to pieces, and I felt so humble and so loving dat I rejoice and praise Got; and now I am resolved to serve Got wit Ned, and Jim, and mine wife, and dese Metodists."

DR. COKE.

"*A burning and a shining light.*"—John.

Dr. Coke was the foreign minister of Methodism. He possessed a zealous and vivacious spirit, which nothing could damp, but which caught inspiration from discouragements, and, like the impeded flood, grew stronger by obstructions. He had marked defects, but is one of the most interesting characters in the history of our church—an example of ministerial zeal worthy of universal admiration and imitation. His stature was low, his voice effeminate, but nis soul was as vast as ever dwelt in a human bosom. He was the first bishop of the Methodist Church in the United States, but found not in a diocese co-extensive with the new world room for his energies. Actuated by an impulse which allowed him no rest, he was perpetually contriving new measures for the extension of the cause which he had embraced. His plans, had he been a man of ordinary abilities, would have entitled him to the character of a visionary fanatic; but he was one of those are spirits whose schemes are but the outline of their grand conceptions, and whose concep-
.ions are the legitimate products of their ener-

gies. He crossed the Atlantic eighteen times at his own expense. Until his death, he had charge of the Methodist missions throughout the world, a work for which he was undoubtedly raised up and qualified by God. He founded the negro missions of the West Indies, which will no doubt exert an important influence on the destiny of those islands. They included fifteen thousand members at the time of his death. He visited the missions which he had established, spent almost the whole of his patrimonial fortune in their support, preached for them, and begged for them from door to door. The missionary spirit was with him "as a burning fire shut up in his bones." When a veteran of almost seventy years, we find him presenting himself before the Wesleyan Conference as a missionary for the East Indies. The conference objected, on account of the expense, when he himself offered to pay the charges of the outfit, to the amount of six thousand pounds. He prevailed over all objections, and embarked with a small band of laborers, died on the voyage, and was buried in the waves; but the undertaking succeeded, and the Wesleyan East India missions are the result. It has been justly asserted that, next to Mr. Wesley, no man was ever connected with the

Wesleyan body who contributed more to extend the blessings of Christianity among mankind. His colleague in the episcopacy of the American church would not allow of even this exception: "A minister of Christ," said Asbury, when the news of his death arrived, "a minister of Christ, in zeal, in labors, and in services, the greatest man of the last century." He has also recorded the sentiment somewhere in his Journal.

Coke was not merely energetic; he possessed a sagacity which was quick in its perceptions, and a comprehension wide in its range. We owe to his judgment some of the most important features in the economy of American Methodism. He first proposed and obtained a permanent establishment of the General Conference to be held at stated times,—a measure which, in giving unity and energy to our vast body, is perhaps unequaled in importance by any other department of our system. In the very outset, his comprehensive mind saw the importance of that provision, the deficiency of which has been, perhaps, our greatest loss, and the supply of which is now so strenuously attempted by us, educational institutions. He had no serious hostility to resist in his efforts for such institutions; but such was the inefficiency, if not indifference, of most others, that the honor of the attempt (and an honor it still is, for it has silenced many a charge against us) belongs almost exclusively to his name. Not discouraged when the first establishment was burned by fire, he pressed with all his energies a second and even more extended attempt, and ceased not his endeavors until he fully succeeded. This institution shared the fate of its predecessor, and (Dr. Coke being mostly absent from the country) Methodism was allowed to grow up without this great auxiliary. What might have been the extent and maturity of Christian education in our land at this moment had the spirit of Coke been more general among us at that period! The intelligent Methodist cannot review the interval of indifference which followed but with mortification and pain, for the immense influence and usefulness which it has subtracted from the church.

Cokesbury College flourished during its shor day with much prosperity. The state legisla ture voluntarily proffered an act of incorporation, with power to confer degrees. Offers were made from Kentucky and Georgia, of land and funds for the founding of similar institutions; a few influential persons pledged two thousand acres of land, and one church subscribed twelve thousand five hundred pounds of tobacco. But the prospect of success which was dawning, and, no doubt, would have opened over the length and breadth of the nation, was disregarded, through an absurd interpretation of one of those providences which, if we may learn from the past, seem preparatory for the success of great plans,—the difficulty of their first operation. It would have been as wise to have abandoned Methodism, because of its first trials, as it was to abandon education because of the conflagration of Cokesbury College.

Dr. Coke was not only useful in the superintendence of great measures—he was active as a preacher; all the minuter duties of a Methodist itinerant, as far as they came within the wide sweep of his ceaseless movements, he performed, and at the same time made no small use of his pen. Wesley used to say he was as a right hand to him. He was unquestionably the next character to Wesley himself in the biographical catalogue of Methodism. It was a noble sentiment recorded by him, at sea, on his first voyage to America, and which illustrates as fully as language can his own character, "I want the wings of an eagle, and the voice of a trumpet, that I may proclaim the gospel through the east and the west, the north and the south."

There is genuine sublimity in the end of this veteran evangelist. Such a man belongs to no locality—he belongs to the world; though dead, his influence is widening daily over the earth, and it was fitting that he should be buried in the ocean, whose waves might sound his requiem on the shores of all lands.

PROGRESS IN PIETY.
" Grow in grace."—Paul.

Is it not the habit of most Christians, after the first fervors of conversion, to content themselves with a uniform practice of the regular duties of religion, maintaining a fixed temper of mind, and expecting no very appreciable advances in piety, except, it may be, in seasons of extraordinary revivals? At least, it is unquestionable that the proportion is very small in the general church, who, in the strong language of David, "pant" after the Lord. The Christian course is represented as a "race." How absurd would it be for a racer to stop at frequent intervals in his progress, or to start with ardor, and then, folding his arms deliberately, *walk* to the goal, as if no prize challenged him and no spectators gazed at him? Do most Christians exemplify the strong language of St. Paul, " Seeing we are compassed about with so great a cloud of witnesses, let us lay aside every weight, and the sin that doth so easily beset us, and let us *run* with patience the race that is set before us ?" What a spectacle would the church exhibit if each member maintained the progressive spirit of his religion! Of course the collective mass would be progressive ; the term revival would become obsolete, for the perpetual spirit of the church would be lively and active. The cultivation of a strenuous piety would inevitably lead to strong sympathy for the unconverted, and the accession to the numbers of the church would be proportionate to the accession to its piety. *The grand characteristic of the millennial church will be the distinct and practical recognition of this principle.* Its approach will be indicated by the growth, and its consummation accomplished by the entire prevalence, of personal piety.

By what means can we make more progress in personal piety ? Is not the first reason of our small progress (first in the order of time as well as in influence) the want of a *definite aim* toward it? It is to be feared that most Christians entertain but a feeble conviction of the *duty* of spiritual progress—of " going on," as St. Paul expresses it. We abandon ourselves to the control of casual circumstances; and are asleep or awake as the influences around us may be dull or quickening. Is not this almost universally the case? Now what would we think of an artisan who should enter his shop and thoughtlessly take up his tools and apply himself indiscriminately to work on whatever materials came first to hand, and pursue this course from day to day until his apartments should be filled with fragments of work, with nothing complete—no definite and final plan? What of an architect who should lay his foundations without reference to the proposed building, or a navigator who should spread his sails alike to all winds, favorable and adverse, contemplating his desired port on his map, but not on his compass? In religion more than anything else we want distinctness, directness. Single out then the particular grace in which you are most deficient, and apply yourself unto it distinctly and daily until you have attained it. You can pray for other blessings, and perform other duties; but let this one be foremost. Think about it, plan for it, bend everything toward it. This advice is applicable not merely to individual graces, but to the great summary blessing of entire sanctification. Whether we attain it gradually or instantaneously, we must address ourselves to its pursuit directly and earnestly, or never obtain it. It is not an accident that may or may not occur in our experience, but an object to be aimed at and labored for.

Again, we should make it a rule in our devotions, especially in prayer, *never to fail to receive immediate and sensible communications from God.* The excellent Mr. Benson maintained this resolution to the last; and those who have read his memoirs know the result. This is entirely a voluntary matter with ourselves. God is always willing to bless us. If we apply to him in faith, nothing can hinder. The rule we now suggest would preserve the mind in a state suited for the ready exercise of faith. How remarkably remiss are we in our most solemn devotions! Would we approach mere human greatness with the same indifference as we do God? Could we converse with an earthly sovereign with the same heartlessness? Would a man beg for his *life,* as we plead for our *souls?* Christian, rouse thyself! Endeavor to feel more fully the reality of the divine presence, especially in the closet. Carry to the place of prayer the purpose *not to cease thine importunity till thou art blessed.* The mere purpose will destroy most of those desultory thoughts which intrude into the sacred retirement, and render its devotions vague and ineffectual.

If Christ were visibly present at the hour of prayer, would we apply to him as we now do? Would not our every word be more direct, more confident? And is he less really present, though invisible? Can we not habituate ourselves to a vivid and immediate realization of his presence? Who will doubt it?

A common reason of our slow progress is our casual habit of reading the Scriptures. We frequently say, but how seldom do we *feel*, that the Scriptures are the word of God? What would be the moral effect of a daily interview with an angel? But what archangel could speak to us as God speaks? If the heavens should open above us only once in our lives, and we behold the excellent glory, and converse with God, would not the scene stamp our whole character? Would we be ordinary men afterward? Would not its brightness, as in the case of Moses on descending from the mount, continue to beam around our persons? But God does converse as infallibly with us in his word. Alas! we do not intently apprehend it. The Scriptures, no doubt, have an immense influence even on the collective mind of communities where they are read, but it is amazing that they do not imbue and dilate more fully individual minds. If the perusal of classic writings is so important for the formation of a vigorous and elegant intellect—if the study of the models of art is so effectual in the improvement of genius—what ought to be the effect of a daily converse with the conceptions of the Infinite Mind? Now, if the classic records, or the celebrated specimens of art, were to be glanced at as slightly, though as habitually, as the Scriptures, would they ever impress their excellences on the susceptibilities of genius? They must be examined; a paragraph or a feature must be studied, thoroughly, laboriously. In like manner should the Scriptures be studied. In studying the models of taste, not only must their import be comprehended by the student, but the spirit, the *anima* which actuates the writer or the artist must be caught—this is the highest attainment of genius. There is much reading, but little studying, of the Scriptures. Our Saviour in his command uses the strongest language, " *Search* the Scriptures."

The point of our remarks is simply that *we should study the word of God daily with express reference to the improvement of our piety.* Such a method, universally used, would develop an efficacy in the truth which would surprise the world. It would not be merely like the efficacy of those occasional circumstances or impulses which we usually depend upon for spiritual improvement, nor merely like that of the hortative addresses of the pulpit. These are all enfeebled by human frailty. It would be potent and sublime from its association with immediate inspiration, and with the purest and grandest truths, such as occupy angel minds. A Christian mind thoroughly conversant with the Scriptures, and accustomed to drink from them as from a fountain of spiritual refreshment, may not manifest such a convulsive zeal, such spasmodic action, as one which depends on impulsive influences; but it will always be more profoundly vigorous, and serenely spiritual, like the deep and steady river in contrast with its tributary stream that leaps and worries down the neighboring hill-side. Search, then, the Scriptures, with the prayer that God would " sanctify you by his truth," and remember that his " word is truth."

Another reason of the small effect of our efforts to advance in religion is frequently the indulgence of some cherished sin. There is no state of mind which will allow of spiritual progress but that in which we are "*pressing* forward. One sin, however apparently insignificant, may interfere with the most powerful influences, as a small object near the eye may exclude the light of the very sun. "*If I regard iniquity in my heart*," says the Psalmist, "*the Lord will not hear me.*" Do you complain, Christian reader, of the barrenness of your soul, of the feeble influence of all the means of grace upon your heart? Pause a moment, and inquire if there is not some neutralizing element, some favored, perhaps concealed sin. Rest not till it is expelled. Remember the struggle is for your soul; that one sin may be your ruin—a taint of depravity which may diffuse itself through your whole spirit, and desolate your whole eternity. Lay aside, therefore, every weight, and the sin that doth so easily beset you, and run with patience the race set before you.

BLACK HARRY OF ST. EUSTATIUS.

"*Weeping may endure for a night: but joy cometh in the morning.*"—Psalmist.

The constant travels and vicissitudes of Dr Coke's life furnished him an exhaustless fund of anecdote, and his social disposition led him to draw on it constantly in company. There is one interesting fact which he often related as an illustration of God's care for both his church and his individual children. Those who heard the doctor preach from the text, "Fear not, little flock," &c., in his flying visits to what were in his day our feeblest societies, may recall the happy illustration, and those who may think it savors too much of fiction will find it authenticated in his private journals and by his biographer.

On the 25th of December, 1786, he was unexpectedly driven by unfavorable winds into the harbor of Antigua, in the West Indies. Actuated by that missionary zeal which allowed him no rest, he immediately began to traverse the islands, preaching wherever he could find opportunity. He arrived at last, with his companion Mr. Hammet, at St. Eustatius, which belonged to the Dutch. As they landed they were addressed by two colored men, who inquired, with a cordiality unusual among strangers, "if they belonged to the brethren." The doctor, supposing they referred to the Moravians, said no, but remarked, that they belonged to the same great spiritual family. The hospitable negroes, however, made no mistake. The doctor was surprised to learn that they had come to welcome him, having received word from the island of St. Christopher's that he designed to visit them. They were two of a number of free negroes who had actually hired a house for his accommodation, which they called his home, and had also provided for the expense of his journey. They conducted him to his new parsonage, where he was entertained with profuse hospitality.

The doctor was taken by surprise. No missionary had been there, and the island was destitute of the means of grace. These generous colored people were evidently children of God: his visit to them was received as that of an angel, and yet there were mingled with their joy signs of a common sorrow. With the utmost interest he inquired into their history. They informed him, in reply, that some months before, a slave named Harry had been brought to the island from the United States, who was converted and had joined a Methodist class before his removal. On arriving among them Harry found himself without a religious associate, and with no means of religious improvement but his private devotions. The poor African nevertheless maintained his fidelity to his Lord. After much anxiety and prayer he began publicly to proclaim to his fellow-servants the name of Christ. Such an example was a great novelty in the island, and attracted much attention. His congregations were large; even the governor of the island deigned to hear him, and, by approving his course, indirectly protected him from the opposition to which his servile condition would otherwise have exposed him.

God owned the labors of his humble servant and at times the Holy Spirit descended in overwhelming influence upon the multitude. Such was the effect on many of the slaves, that they fell like dead men to the earth, and lay for hours insensible. At a meeting not long before the doctor's arrival, sixteen persons were thus struck down under his exhortations. Such an extraordinary circumstance excited a general sensation among the planters. They determined to suppress the meetings. They appealed to the governor, who immediately ordered the slave before him, and forbade his preaching by severe penalties. So far had the planters succeeded in exciting the morose temper of the governor, that it was only by the intervention of the supreme Judge that Harry was saved from being cruelly flogged. His faithful labors were now peremptorily stopped. It was a remarkable coincidence that Dr. Coke arrived the very day on which Harry was silenced; hence the mingled joy and sorrow of the "little flock" who so hospitably entertained him.

After giving the doctor this information, they insisted upon his preaching to them immediately, lest by delay the opportunity should be lost; but fearing, from the silence which had that day been imposed on Harry, that it might result in more evil than good, he declined until he should see the governor. Such, however, was their hunger for the bread of life, that he could not induce them to separate till they had twice sung, and he had thrice joined with them in prayer.

The doctor found, by his interview with the authorities, that it would be imprudent to tarry on the island. He therefore formed the little persecuted band into classes under the most prudent man he could find among them, and, committing them to God, departed amid their tears and prayers. So amply had they supplied him with fruits and other provisions, that in a voyage of near three weeks, during which eight persons shared these bounties with him, they were not exhausted.

Poor Harry, suspected and watched, did not presume to preach again ; but supposing, after a considerable interval, that the excitemen against him had ceased, and that the prohibition only extended to his preaching, he ventured to pray openly with his brethren. He was immediately summoned before the governor, and sentenced to be publicly whipped, then imprisoned, and afterward banished from the island. The sentence was executed with unrelenting cruelty. but the poor negro felt himself honored in suffering for his Master. While the blood streamed from his back, his Christian fortitude was unshaken. From the whipping-post he was taken to prison, whence he was secretly removed, but whither none of his little company could discover.

In 1789 Dr. Coke returned to the West Indies. After preaching at many other islands, he again visited St. Eustatius to comfort its suffering society. The spirit of persecution still raged there, and the fate of Harry was still wrapped in impenetrable mystery. None of his associates had been able to obtain the slightest information respecting him since his disappearance. A cruel edict had been passed by the local government, inflicting thirty-nine lashes on any colored man who should be found praying. It seemed the determination of the authorities to banish religion from the island; yet the seed sown by Harry had sprung up, and nothing could uproot it. During all these trials the little society of St. Eustatius had been growing, its persecuted members had contrived, by some means, to preserve their union, and the doctor found them two hundred and fifty-eight strong, and privately baptized many before his departure. They had been, indeed, " hid with Christ in God." The government again drove him from the island.

After visiting the United States and England, this tireless man of God was, in 1790, again sounding the alarm among the West India Islands, and again he visited St. Eustatius. A new governor had been appointed, and he hoped for a better reception, but he was repelled as obstinately as before. Still the great Shepherd took care of the flock. The rigor of the laws against them had been somewhat relaxed, and, in the providence of God, eight exhorters had arisen among them, who were extensively useful to the slaves. To these and to the leaders he gave private advice and comfort, and, committing them to God, who had hitherto so marvelously kept them, he again departed. The chief care of the society devolved on a person named Ryley, who, about four years previously, had been converted under the labors of black Harry. Harry's fate was still involved in mysterious secrecy, and his friends indulged the worst fears. But his "works followed him;" he had kindled a fire in St. Eustatius which many waters could not quench. On his return to England Dr. Coke interested the Wesleyan churches in his behalf, and many were the prayers which ascended for him and the afflicted church which he had planted.

In 1792 the doctor again visited the island, but he was not allowed to preach. Nothing was yet known of the fate of poor Harry. The spirit of persecution still prevailed, and even feeble women had been dragged to the whipping-post for having met for prayer. But, in the good providence of God, religion still prospered secretly, and the classes met by stealth. The doctor left them with a determination to go to Holland and solicit the interposition of the parent government. This he did with his usual perseverance, but not with success. The tyranny of the local government continued about twelve years longer; but the great Head of the church at last sent deliverance to his people. In 1804, about eighteen years after Harry was silenced, a missionary was admitted to the island; a chapel was afterward built and Sunday schools established, and St. Eustatius has since continued to be named among the successful missions of the West Indies. Dr. Coke lived to see this long-closed door opened, and the devoted missionary enter with the bread of life for the famishing, but faithful little band of disciples.

Thus does the providence of God protect those who put their trust in him. "Weeping may endure for a night, but joy cometh in the morning." God will, sooner or later, help those who help themselves.

But what became of poor Harry? During about ten years his fate was unknown, and all hope of discerning it before the sea should give up its dead was abandoned. About this time the doctor again visited the States. One evening, after preaching, he was followed to his room by a colored man, deeply affected. It was poor black Harry! Reader, what would you not have given to witness that interview? He had been sent in a cargo of slaves to the States, but was now free. Through all these years and changes he had "kept the faith," and was still exercising himself with continued usefulness in the sphere which he occupied.

THE WAY OF LIFE.

"He that believeth shall be saved."—Christ.

How plain is the way of life; how explicit is the statement of the plan of salvation! " By grace are ye saved through faith; and that not of yourselves; it is the gift of God, not of works, lest any man should boast." The apostle affirms, first, the great proposition of salvation, "*ye are saved;*" secondly, the primary cause of it, "*grace;*" and thirdly, the instrumental cause, "*faith:*" and how carefully he guards against Pelagian confidence, " Not of yourselves, it is the gift of God;" and again he repeats it, " not of works, lest any man should boast." It would seem impossible to mistake the universal import of the New Testament on this its ostensible topic, but how many misapprehend it!—how many grope through long lives down to the grave with the Bible in their hands, ignorant of its first principle, and never knowing that *peace in believing* which is its balm for the heart's wretchedness! The churches of whole lands have lost sight of the doctrine of justification by faith; lands, too, profoundly skilled in Scriptural exegesis. Alas, for the perversity of man! Though pervaded with depravity, dead in trespasses and sins, miserable and lost, yet would he presume to confront the throne of his Judge with pretences of merit.

Such were my reflections as I descended from the chamber of an individual whose life was flickering with consumption, like the expiring taper in its socket, and whose only solace for the future was the reflection that he had been just to his fellow-men. As his is not an uncommon case, its introduction here may be useful to others.

On taking a seat by his bed, I expressed my sympathy for his sufferings, and my hope that they were working out for him a far more exceeding and eternal weight of glory.

He hesitated in his answer, and remarked that "death was dreadful to a man under any circumstances."

"And yet," said I, "'the sting of death is sin;' and Paul exclaims, 'O death, where is thy sting? O grave, where is thy victory?

Thanks be to God, who giveth *us* the victory, through our Lord Jesus Christ.' The primitive Christians seemed to anticipate it as altogether desirable. The same apostle says expressly, ' I *desire* to depart and be with Christ ;' and he represents the Corinthian brethren as ' willing rather to be absent from the body and to be present with the Lord ;' nay, as ' groaning' in ' this tabernacle,' ' earnestly desiring to be clothed upon with their house which is from heaven.'"

"Yes," replied the sick man ; "but the church is not now what it then was. Still, God is merciful. I place my trust in him. I have endeavored to live honestly, and I hope I shall die in peace."

I was startled at his defective views, for he had been the child of religious parents, and had faithfully observed the external duties of religion. I endeavored to convince him of the depravity of the heart, and its utter unfitness for heaven without faith in Christ and the renewal of the Holy Ghost. My reasonings were evidently heard with reluctance, but I hoped with effect, and, praying for the blessing of the Spirit upon them, I took my leave, designing to call again after allowing him sufficient time for reflection.

He was born and educated in Massachusetts. With a strictly Puritan morality, he united the practical tact, general intelligence, and not a little of the metaphysical acuteness of New-England. At my first visit he showed quite a propensity to rebut my appeals by logical difficulties. It was my ardent prayer, as I went to his chamber the next day, that the Lord would enable me to strip from him that guise of self-righteousness which, instead of the wedding garment, is the winding sheet of the soul, one, alas! in which many a self-deluded sinner has laid down in eternal death. I perceived immediately that my former conversation had produced an effect. He seemed anxious and inquisitive, but still unwilling to abandon his false reliance.

"But do you not think, sir," said he, "that an honest man will be saved?"

"Yes, a truly honest man, honest toward God as well as man, he who honestly conforms to God's terms of salvation; not one who is honest only according to the moral standard of the world, but he who lives by faith, for 'by grace ye are saved through faith; and that not of yourselves; it is the gift of God, not of works, lest any man should boast,' and 'he that believeth not shall be damned.'"

"But can there be much difference between strict morality and piety?"

"The difference is vast. Look at a few particulars. Morality, so called, in its highest form, proposes nothing but *present* and *future* uprightness. True religion proposes this, but also the pardon of the *past*. The strictest moralist will admit that he has sinned in the past, but he makes no provision for past sin. Utter rectitude in the present and the future is no more than his duty; it can involve no supererogative merit which might be transferred to the past. What hope has he, then? The fatal plague spot, however small, is upon him. One sin introduced 'death and all our wo;' one sin unforgiven is a spring which, touched by the hand of death, will throw all his eternal destinies into ruin. The Christian has a provision for the past, for he believes in 'him whom God hath set forth to be a propitiation through faith in his blood, to declare his righteousness for the remission of sins that are past.'

"Again. Morality is generally limited to relative duties, those which are mutual among men; these form but one class of duties, and though an important, yet a secondary class Man has a higher relation than that which binds him to his fellows; he is related to God, and this relation involves duties; the duties of filial love, of prayer, of praise, and all acts of spiritual devotion. The moralist prides himself on his fidelity to man, while he recklessly refuses the higher claims of God. What though he commits no positive sin against society, yet he is every moment guilty of negative sins against God. And negative sins may be as guilty as positive ones. Positive crimes appear to us more enormous because recognized and punished by human law; but who can say that to refuse to love or worship God is not as great a sin, nay, greater than theft or murder? I do not say it is, but who can assert it is not? What, then, is the character of the man who has been all his life incurring such guilt? How can he enter the presence of his insulted God?

"And then look at the sentiments which usually accompany morality. How do they contrast with those of true *religion*? They are sentiments of pride, of honor, so called. Like the Pharisee in the temple, the moralist flatters himself that he is not like other men. Not so the Christian: he feels himself to be the chief of sinners; of himself he is but weakness and guiltiness. And yet, while he knows that of himself he can do nothing, there is within him a sublime consciousness of power, the indwelling Godhead, and he feels that he can do all things through Christ, which strengtheneth him.

"Morality is a self-imposed virtue; true religion is the renewal of the heart by the Holy Ghost received by faith. It is 'the life of God in the soul of man.' Lean not, then, my dear friend, on this broken reed. You are hastening to your end; look to the Lamb of God, which taketh away the sins of the world. He is your only hope."

With tears in his eyes, the sick man replied, "O that I had given my attention to these things earlier! I would do right, I wish to be honest with myself. I have not been satisfied with my condition, and every hour it grows more doubtful. Your arguments appear correct, and yet I am perplexed to know why so much importance is attached to faith—why all the hopes and promises of religion are suspended on it."

"It should be a sufficient answer," I replied, "that Infinite Wisdom has seen fit so to construct the economy of salvation, and therefore the reasons for the fact, however mysterious to us, must be important. But there are many considerations which give an obvious propriety to this peculiarity of the Christian system.

"A religion which should not provide for the practical improvement of its followers would be of little advantage to the world; and yet one that should make the hope of salvation dependent upon practical duties would be but a ministry of condemnation, especially to all who, by advanced years, or sickness, or sudden death, are placed beyond the reach of the self-discipline of active virtue; it would likewise tend to its own destruction, by giving occasion to the self-dependence and self-righteousness of those who receive it. Now the gospel avoids this liability by making salvation dependent entirely on a principle which involves no merit in itself, but tacitly ascribes it all to God, and yet *implies such a frame of mind as necessarily will produce the exercise of every practical virtue.* Faith, by implying the absence of all self-dependence, produces humility; by reposing all its dependence on God leads to gratitude and love, and gratitude and love lead to adoration; and, like the filial dependence and love of the child to the parent, they lead also to all obedience and faithfulness. Works have therefore properly been called the evidences of faith. The two most appropriate sentiments to the human mind are kept in lively exercise by faith, namely, the exaltation of God and abasement of self. God's goodness, and our own utter inability, are perpetually suggested by it. Its exercise is direct communion with God. If we were to be saved by the secondary instrumentality of works, we might forget God in our attention to subordinate means; but faith is an application directly to his throne, and brings us into the light of his excellent glory.

"How admirably is Christianity thus adapted to what must always be the great object of true religion, the improvement, the moral discipline of man, and by a process, too, which to the superficial eye of the skeptic appears calculated to do away the force of moral duties! Indeed, the more the great doctrine of the atonement is scrutinized, the more manifest are its claims to be called the wisdom and the power of God. What form of truth could be better suited than this for all the purposes of pure and spiritual religion? What one could more exalt God and improve man? What one could more fully dignify the justice of the divine throne, and yet crown with mercy and hope the most dangerous emergency of the penitent sinner? What one could better meet your own case, my dear friend? Is it not what you need? and will you not embrace it? O believe and be saved."

Seldom have I seen a more affecting expression of self-abandonment, and anxiety, hope, and humility, than was presented by this poor invalid at the close of the conversation. The Spirit of God was evidently striving with him. With weeping eyes and the tenderness of a child, he exclaimed, "O, sir, this is just what I need. I am standing between both worlds and in all the universe around me I see but one object upon which I can fix my eyes with confidence, and that is the cross. I tremble even as I look at that symbol of love and mercy. O, can it be that I may be saved?"

I conversed with him longer, and commended him to the grace of God in prayer.

For more than a week after this visit I was absent at conference, leaving my charge in the care of a local preacher, who visited him daily. During one of these calls he received peace in believing, and had since been daily sinking under disease, but rejoicing in hope of the glory of God. On my return I immediately visited him. He was not expected to survive the day. His utterance was difficult, but his mind glowed with that brilliancy and vigor which so often accompany this fatal, but gentle disease. His late, but complete change, was a remarkable instance of the power of grace, and the Lord deigned to him a triumphant exit. It would be interesting to give the details of his final experience; but my design has been to show the fallacy of his erroneous views, and this outline has already extended too far. Let it suffice to say, that the grace which had thus remarkably rescued him cheered with increasing consolation his remaining hours. I penciled a few of his dying sentences.

"How astonishing was my delusion! how different my life now looks! guilt—guilt—guilt—all is guilt. I am a brand plucked from the burning. I am saved on the very threshold of hell."

"O that I had more strength to praise Him! My time is so short, and so little of it has been devoted to Him, I want to testify his wonderful mercy every instant."

"I cannot fear; his boundless grace surrounds and sustains me. Well did the Psalmist call it the 'valley of the shadow of death.' It is but a *shadow*, a shade in a refreshing valley."

"I would not exchange this dying bed for the throne of a monarch; all my trust is in God, and I could now trust him, though all fallen spirits should gather about me. I am going, going, going to my Lord and Saviour; though at the eleventh hour, I am saved. I am saved Let none hereafter despair."

With similar expressions, he lingered about

two hours, and then sweetly fell asleep in Jesus. "He that believeth shall be saved." Blessed be God, the truth has never failed.

ORIGIN OF THE METHODIST ECONOMY.

"God hath chosen the weak things of the world to confound the mighty."—Paul.

The origin of Methodism has always appeared to me a remarkable chapter in the history of Providence, and its economy one of the most remarkable passages in that chapter.

Time has proved it to be the most efficient of all modern religious organizations, not only among the dispersed population of a new country, but also in the dense community of an ancient people; on the American frontier, and in the English city, it is found efficacious beyond all other plans, stimulating, impelling all others, and yet outstripping them.

This wonderful system of religious instrumentalities was not conceived *a priori*. It was not the result of sagacious foresight; it grew up spontaneously. Its elementary parts were evolved unexpectedly in the progress of the sect. Wesley saw that the state of religion throughout the English nation required a thorough reform; and "felt in himself," says Southey, "the power and the will for it, both in such plenitude, that they appeared to him a manifestation not to be doubted of the will of Heaven." He looked not into the future, but consulted only the openings of present duty. "Whither," says the same author, "they were to lead he knew not, nor what form of consistence the societies he was collecting would assume, nor where he was to find laborers as he enlarged the field of his operations, nor how the scheme was to derive its temporal support. But these considerations neither troubled him, nor made him for a moment foreslacken his course. God, he believed, had appointed it, and God would always appoint means for his own ends."

He expected at first to keep within the restrictions of the national Church, to which he was devotedly attached. The manner in which he was providentially led to adopt, one by one, the peculiar measures which at last consolidated into a distinct and unparalleled system, is an interesting feature in the history of Methodism Let us trace it a moment.

The doctrines which he preached, and the novel emphasis with which he preached them, led to his expulsion from the pulpits of the

Establishment. This, together with the immense assemblies he attracted, compelled him to proclaim them *in the open air*—a measure which the moral wants of the country demanded, and which is justified, as well by the example of Christ as by its incalculable results.

The inconvenience of the "rooms" occupied by his followers for spiritual meetings at Bristol led to the erection of a more commodious edifice. This was a place of occasional preaching, then of regular worship, and finally, without the slightest anticipation of such a result, the first in *a series of chapels* which became the habitual resort of his followers, and thereby contributed, more, perhaps, than any other cause, to their organization into a distinct sect.

The debt incurred by this building rendered necessary *a plan of contribution* among those who assembled in it. They agreed to pay a penny a week. They were divided into companies of twelve, one of whom, called the leader, was appointed to receive their contributions. At their weekly meetings for the payment of this small sum, they found leisure for religious conversation and prayer. These companies, formed thus for a local and temporary object, were afterward called *classes*, and the arrangement was incorporated into the regular economy of Methodism. In this manner originated one of the most distinctive features of our system—our classes—the advantages of which are beyond all estimation. The class meeting has, more than any other means, preserved our original purity. It is the best school of experimental divinity the world has ever seen. It has given a sociality of spirit and a disciplinary training to Methodism which are equaled in no other sect.

We cannot but admire the providential adaptation of this institution to another which was subsequently to become all-important in our economy—I mean an *itinerant ministry*. Such a ministry could not admit of much pastoral labor, especially in the new world, where the circuits were long. The class leader became a substitute for the preacher in this department of his office. The fruits of an itinerant ministry must have disappeared in many, perhaps most places, during the long intervals which elapsed between the visits of the earlier preachers, had they not been preserved by the class meeting. A small class has been the germ of almost every church we have formed. It was the germ from which has developed the whole growth of our vast cause, for it was *the first organic form of Methodism.*

Another most important result of the class meetings, formed so accidentally, or rather providentially, at Bristol, was the pecuniary provision they led to for the prosecution of the plans which were daily enlarging under the hands of Wesley. The whole *fiscal system* of Methodism arose from the Bristol penny collections. Thus, without foreseeing the great independent cause he was about to establish, Wesley formed, through a slight circumstance, a simple and yet most complete system of finance for the immense expenses which its future prosecution would involve. And how admirably was this pecuniary system adapted to the circumstances of that cause! He was destined to raise up a vast religious combination; it was to include the *poorer* classes, and yet require *large* pecuniary resources. How were these resources to be provided among a poor people? The project presents a complete dilemma. The providential formation of a plan of finance which suited the poverty of the poorest, and which worldly sagacity would have contemned, banished all difficulty, and has led to pecuniary results which have surprised the world.

That other important peculiarity of our church already alluded to, *a lay and itinerant ministry*, was equally providential in its origin. Wesley was at first opposed to the employment of lay preachers. He expected the co-operation of the regular clergy. They, however, were his most hostile antagonists. Meanwhile, the small societies formed by his followers for spiritual improvement increased. "What," says he, "was to be done in a case of so extreme necessity, where so many souls lay at stake? No clergyman would assist at all. The expedient that remained was to seek some one among themselves who was upright of heart and of sound judgment in the things of God, and to desire him to meet the rest as often as he could, to confirm them, as he was able, in the ways of God, either by reading to them, or by prayer or exhortation." This was the origin of the Methodist *lay ministry*.

The multiplication of societies exceeded the increase of preachers. This rendered it necessary that the latter should itinerate, and thence arose the *Methodist itinerancy*. Our itinerancy is the most admirable feature in our whole ministerial system. It is not a labor-saving provision—it is the contrary of this—but it is truly a laborer-saving one. The pastoral service, which otherwise would have been confined to a single parish, is extended by this plan to scores, and sometimes hundreds, of towns and villages and, by the co-operation of the class meeting, is rendered almost as efficient as it would be were it local. It is this peculiarity that has rendered our ministry so successful in our new states. It has also contributed, perhaps, more than any other cause, to maintain a sentiment of unity among us. It gives a pilgrim character to our preachers. They feel that "here they have no abiding city," and are led more earnestly to "seek one" out of sight. It will not allow them to entangle themselves with local trammels. The cross peculiarly "crucifies them to the world, and the world to them." Their zeal, rising into religious chivalry; their devotion to one work; their disregard for ease and the conveniences of stationary life,—are owing, under divine grace, chiefly to their itinerancy. It has made them one of the most self-sacrificing, laborious, practical, and successful bodies of men at present to be found in the great field of Christian labor. The time when itinerancy shall cease in our ministry, and classes among our laity, will be the date of our downfall.

METHODISM ADAPTED TO OUR COUNTRY

"The wilderness and the solitary place shall be glad for them: and the desert shall rejoice, and blossom as the rose."—Isaiah.

There is another and no less interesting light in which the economy of Methodism strikes me as providential; I mean its *adaptation to our country*. It is a fact worthy of remark, that while the great moral revolution of Methodism was going on across the Atlantic, the greatest political revolution of modern times was in process on our own continent; and when we contemplate the new adaptations of religious action which were evolved by the former, we cannot resist the conviction that there was a providential relation between the two events—that they were not only coincident in time, but also in purpose. While Wesley and his co-laborers were reviving Christianity there, Washington and his compatriots were reviving liberty here. It was the American Revolution that led to the development of the resources of this vast country, and rendered it the assembling place of all nations, kindreds, tongues, and people; and Methodism commenced its operations sufficiently early to be in good vigor by the time that the great movement of the civilized world toward the West began. It seems to have been divinely adapted to this emergency of our country. If we may judge from the result, it was raised up by Providence more in reference to the new than to the old world. Its peculiar measures were strikingly suited to the circumstances of the country, while those of every other contemporary sect were as strikingly unadapted to them. Its zealous spirit readily blended with the buoyant sympathies of a youthful nation flushed with the sense of liberty. The usual process of a long preparatory training for the ministry could not consist with the rapidly-increasing wants of the country. Methodism called into existence a ministry less trained, but not less efficient; possessing in a surprising degree that sterling good sense and manly energy, examples of which great exigences always produce among the people. These it imbued with its own quenchless spirit, and formed them to a standard of character altogether unique in the annals of mankind; they composed a class which, perhaps, will never be seen again They were distinguished for native mental vigor, shrewdness, extraordinary knowledge of human nature, many of them for overwhelming natural eloquence, the effects of which on popular assemblies are scarcely paralleled in the history of ancient or modern oratory; and not a few for powers of satire and wit, which made the gainsayer cower before them. To these intellectual attributes they added extraordinary excellences of the heart, a zeal which only burned more fervently where that of most men would have grown faint, a courage that exulted in perils, a deep tenderness for the poor and suffering, a generosity which knew no bounds, and which left most of them in want in their latter days, a forbearance and co-operation with each other which are seldom found in large bodies, an utter devotion to one work, and, withal, a simplicity of character which extended to their manners and their apparel. They were likewise characterized by wonderful physical abilities. They were mostly robust. The feats of labor and endurance which they performed in incessantly preaching in the village and in the "city full," in the slave hut and the Indian wigwam; in journeyings, interrupted by no stress of weather; in fording creeks, swimming rivers, sleeping in forests;—these, with the novel circumstances with which such a career must frequently bring them into collision would afford examples of life and character which, in the hands of genius, might be the materials for a new department of romantic literature. They were men who labored as if the judgment fires had already broken out on the world, and time was to end with their day These were precisely the men which the moral wants of the new world, at the time we are contemplating, demanded.

The usual plan of local labor, limited to a single congregation or to a parish, was inadequate to the wants of Great Britain at this time; but much more so to those of the new continent. That extraordinary conception of Wesley, an itinerant ministry, met in the only manner possible the circumstances of the latter; and the men whom we have described were the only characters who could have carried out this gigantic conception. No one can estimate what would have been the probable result of that rapid advance which the population of the United States was making beyond the customary provisions for religious instruction, had not this novel plan met the emergency. Much of what was then our frontier, but since has become the most important states of the Union, would have passed through the forming period of its character without the influence of Christian institutions. But the Methodist itinerancy has borne the cross, not only in the midst, but in the van, of the hosts of emigration. That *beau ideal* of hardship, disinterestedness, and romantic adventure, the Methodist itinerant, is found with his horse and saddle-bags threading the trail of the savage, and cheering and blessing with his visits the loneliest cottage on the furthest frontier. They have gone as pioneers to the aboriginal tribes, and have gathered into the pale of the church more of the children of the forest than any other sect; they have scaled the Rocky Mountains, and are building up Christianity and civilization on the shores of the Columbia; they are hastening down toward the capital of Montezuma, while, throughout the length and breadth of our older states, they have been spreading a healthful influence which has affected all classes, so that their cause includes not only a larger aggregate population than any other sect, but especially a larger proportion of those classes whose moral elevation is the most difficult and the most important,—the savage, the slave, the free negro, and the lower classes generally.

The complex and yet harmonious constitution of the Methodist Church in the United States would be an interesting subject of discussion. It is a vast system of wheels within wheels, but all revolving with the ease of a well-made machine. Our general conferences occurring once in four years, the annual conferences once a year, the quarterly conferences once in three months, the leaders' meetings once a month, the classes once a week, form an admirable series of gradations extending from a week to four years, and covering all the successive intervals. To these correspond also our gradations of labor,—bishops traversing the continent, presiding elders traveling over extended districts, circuit preachers occupying less extensive fields, assisted by local preachers and exhorters; and finally, leaders inspecting, weekly, divisions of the local societies. This exact machinery is the secret of the energy and permanence of so diffuse and varied a system. And was it not providential that such a system was raised up at such a time?

THE HOSPITABLE WIDOW AND THE TRACT.

"*Cast thy bread upon the waters, for thou shalt find it after many days.*"—Solomon.

The day of judgment alone can reveal the amount of good accomplished by the humble instrumentality of tracts. God's word is the "tree of life," but tracts are its leaves—the leaves which are for the "healing of the nations." Cheap, brief, and pithy statements of religious truth—cheap, that they may be multiplied and scattered broadcast; brief, that they may be read in the moments of leisure which the laboring man can snatch from his toil, and pithy, that they may be read with interest and profit—such publications ought to fall, like pure snow flakes, on all lands. Like the fall of the blossom leaves, they would be followed by fruit in due season. If we cannot give whole loaves, let us multiply by breaking them, and scatter the fragments, at least.

I could fill this volume with illustrations of their utility. I will give, however, but one fact, another example of the usefulness of Dr. Coke.*

---
* This anecdote is authenticated in one of the Reports of the English Religious Tract Society.

This indefatigable servant of Christ was traveling once in what was then a wilderness part of our country. At that time there were few bridges, but to swim streams was a small feat with the hardy pioneers of Methodism and their well-trained steeds. It was an exploit, however, to which the good doctor and his horse were not accustomed. A river lay in his course, and he endeavored, by an indirect route, to cross it at the ford, but missed the place. Impatient to proceed, and ambitious to equal the achievements of his American brethren, he patted the neck of his horse, and plunged into the flood. The water was deep, and the horse becoming alarmed, began to struggle and sink, to the imminent peril of his rider. The doctor, extricating his feet from the stirrups, seized on an overhanging bough, and, after being thoroughly drenched, reached the shore, to which the affrighted animal had also returned.

He remained in the forest till he had dried his clothes in the sun, and then mounted to return. On the road he met a man who directed him to the nearest village, and gave him the address of a kind family, where he might expect to be hospitably entertained as an ambassador of God. The doctor, as usual, gave him a hearty word of exhortation and rode on, wearied with the fatigues of the day, but happy in the expectation of a cordial reception and comfortable rest in the neighboring hamlet.

Early in the evening he arrived at the village, and was received with all kindness by the good lady of the house to which he had been directed. The table was spread with a bountiful meal, and after his usual domestic service, which consisted in an appropriate exhortation, besides the Scripture lesson and prayer, he retired to rest, thankful to God for so comfortable a conclusion to the trials of the day. The next morning he took an early leave of the family, addressing to each some spiritual counsel, and leaving behind him a single tract, for at that day these convenient little vehicles of truth were rare and precious, and the few who distributed them were obliged to make the most of them.

The doctor returned to England, visited Ireland and the West Indies, traversing, as usual, land and sea in the cause of his Master. After five years had passed away, he was again on the American continent. On his way to one of the conferences, he overtook a number of the preachers who were journeying thither. They all hailed their old friend and bishop with hearty congratulations; but one young man who accompanied them was deeply affected at the unexpected meeting, and was observed to wipe the tears from his eyes. When they had rode several miles, the young man contrived to get by the side of the doctor, and on inquiring if he recollected being in a certain part of America about five years ago, he answered in the affirmative.

"And do you recollect, sir, being nearly drowned in trying to cross a river?"

"I remember it quite well."

"And do you remember spending the night at the cottage of a widow lady in such a village?"

"Indeed I do," said the doctor, "and I shall not soon forget the kindness shown me by that excellent family."

"And do you remember that you presented a tract to the lady when you departed the next morning?"

"I do not recall that," replied the doctor, "but as I do so often, it is quite possible I did so then."

"Well, sir, you did leave there a tract, which that lady still keeps, and if you ever pass through the village again you can see it; but no money can purchase it from her. She read it, and the Lord made it the instrument of her conveision; a number of her children and her neighbors have also been converted through its instrumentality, and there is now in the village a prosperous society."

"God be praised," exclaimed the doctor, and the tears gushed in a flood from his eyes.

The young man weeping, also, proceeded,— "I have not quite reported all yet. I am one of the sons of that widow, and I shall ever bless God for that tract, for by reading it, my feet were directed in the way to heaven, and I am now going to conference to be proposed as a traveling preacher. My saddle-bags are half full of tracts, and I shall ever carry them with me, and scatter them in my course."

Reader, though you may consider yourself the feeblest child of God, here is a potent means of good which you can use daily. Have you small talents? Can you not speak with readiness for your Lord? Then carry with you these little messages of truth. Let them speak in your stead. You may thus scatter seed that may bring forth fruit, "some a hundred-fold some sixty, some thirty."

MY LIBRARY.

" On booke for to rede I me delite,
And to them give I faith and full credence,
And in my heart have them in reverence."—Chaucer.

In all my changes I have kept sacredly my books. They are not two hundred in number, great and small, but include good specimens of the most valuable classes: How many happy hours do I owe them! In many a long journey, on horseback, in the wilderness, have I beguiled the weary day by converse with a favorite author; and now that infirmities have compelled me to retire from my Master's work, these fast friends still cleave to me in my solitude, comforting and enlivening it by their instructive companionship. In sickness they nave relieved me more than medicine, in sorrow they have been my solace, and in poverty my riches; and now, as I sit penning these lines, they are round about me, looking like the familiar faces of old friends, full of love, tried and true. "Blessed be God," said one, "for books;" and "they are not wise," said another, "who object to much reading." Like the men who write them, they are of all characters, but we may select them as we choose our friends;

and when once we select good ones, unlike men, they vary not, but are steadfast in their integrity.

I can never be solitary with good books about me; a blessed society are they, ready at any moment to listen to our inquiries, and entertain us with their tranquil converse. By biographies, I can assemble round my winter hearth the men whose thoughts have stirred nations and impelled ages. While living, their company and conversations were enjoyed only by those who moved in the same sphere of life; but in books they obey my bidding, and divested of those forms of life which would only have embarrassed me, they become familiar friends, and teach me the lessons of their wisdom.

I have a few volumes of history. They crowd ages of existence into my evening hours; fields, cities, realms, with their armies, arts, and revolutions, pass before me, within my humble walls, like a magnificent drama.

I have books of travel. Though their authors are in their graves, I have only to open their pages, when, as by magic, they appear before me; and I attend with breathless interest to the recital of their voyages, their adventures, the countries they visited, and all the scenes of novelty and marvel they witnessed. Thus in few hours I sail over seas, and travel over continents, enjoying all the pleasures and suffering none of the perils of the journey.

I have a few good volumes of poetry. The language of harmony and the bright ideals of genius are addressed by them to the deepest susceptibilities of my heart.

I have books of religion. In them, men who have gone up to heaven still instruct me in the way thither, and console me in the trials of my pilgrimage. And, above all, in my Bible I have an exhaustless treasure—the most simple and beautiful construction of the English language, the richest poetry, the most graphic portraits, the most interesting history, and the purest truth. Kings, prophets, and apostles move before me, and the visions and voices of the invisible world come down upon my soul.

If there were but one copy of any of the great literary works extant, one Paradise Lost, one Pilgrim's Progress, or, above all, one Bible, how would it be prized! What treasure would not be given for it! How happy would be esteemed the possessor! But are they less a blessing, because they may be obtained by the humblest man?

With such solace from books, it is not surprising that the love of reading, like the physical appetites, grows by indulgence, and frequently assumes the intensity of a passion. "A taste for books," says Gibbon, "is the pleasure and glory of my life. I would not exchange it for the wealth of the Indies." Cicero says that he occupied himself with books at "home and abroad, in the city and the country, walking and riding." Pliny says that even in hunting, he employed his intervals in reading. And our earliest poet, Chaucer, has expressed a still stronger passion:

> "But as for me, although I can but lite,*
> On booke for to rede I me delite,
> And to them give I faithe and full credence,
> And in my heart have them in reverence;
> So heartily that there is game none
> That from my bookes meketh me to gone."

Thus books are sources of genuine *pleasure*. The mind, like the body, is formed for activity. In higher studies, its activity, though profitable, is laborious and painful, like the physical toil which excavates the golden mine; but in miscellaneous reading, while it is not without profit, it is also easy and delightful, like the pleasurable exercise of a walk amid the fresh breezes, the bright light, the varied charms of the landscape. As a relaxation from manual toil,

* Know but little.

what can be more delicious than good books? In them the manifest scenes of life are painted, the affections of the heart are embalmed, the creations of the imagination are pictured, the gorgeous pageants of history revolve, the beauties of nature and the wonders of art are exhibited, the noblest thoughts of the noblest minds, the best sentiments of the best hearts, are treasured.

Books are our best companions. They change not, they forsake us not. They furnish us always the same faithful and sincere instructions. They are friends with whom we can converse in the loneliest solitude; and often have they gladdened the spirit of genius amid the damps of the prison cell, and the wretchedness of the garret. Well could the immortal author of the " Faerie Queene," in the neglect and want of his latter years, sing,—

> "However men may me despise and spite,
>   I feed on such contentment of good thought,
> And please myself with mine own self-delight,
>   In contemplating things heavenly wrought;
> And loathing earth, I look to yonder sky,
> And being driven hence, I thither fly."

Books are the prime means of *intellectual improvement*, and no insignificant instruments of *moral* influence. Various reading has been condemned as unfavorable to mental vigor and originality. It has been said that perhaps the ancients owed much of their excellence to the fact, that they had fewer books than we, and, therefore, read less and thought more; and even in their scarcity of literary works, one of them advised the studious youth of Rome to read much, but read *few* books. The advice is certainly pertinent, but may be much qualified. It is unquestionable that the most powerful minds have been distinguished for extensive research. Fisher Ames said that the largest library in the United States, in his day, did not equal the number of works referred to as authorities in Gibbon's "Decline and Fall." Some of the most distinguished English writers have been various and voracious readers. Bacon was a great reader as well as a great observer and thinker, and his own quaint remark suggests the manner in which he avoided any evil from the indulgence; "Some books," said he, "are to be tasted, some swallowed, and some few chewed and digested." Not only do individual instances confirm the position, but the most intellectual nation of the age presents an example of the most various and minute research, combined with the most profound originality. Bibliomania is the very genius of a German student. Nature has provided an endless variety for the nourishment of man, and it is not the meagre and unvarying use of her blessings which invigorates; the healthy may enjoy them abundantly, provided they be seasonable and temperate.

But however strong may be the objections to the miscellaneous use of books by professed students, they do not apply to the popular mind. The mass of the people have neither the disposition nor the convenience for mental *discipline*. With them there is but one alternative,—either to reap the slight improvements, but genuine pleasures, of occasional and desultory reading, or suffer the inanition or worse accompaniments of an habitual neglect of books. But though their improvement by such a course be but slight, compared with the effects of systematic study, yet, in itself considered, it is vast. The inert faculties are awakened; the tendency of the uniform and minutely-divided mechanic arts to stint the mind is relieved; the delightful instinct of taste is called into play; the languid imagination is vivified, and the judgment exercised. A mechanic, who is accustomed to spend an hour or two daily in judicious reading, will show its effects in his whole bearing. It may awaken within him no peculiar energy, it may impart no new talent, but it will give a better tone to his ordinary powers, and greater purity to his common sentiments; and it will, almost invariably, so far modify his whole character, as to distinguish him from the mass of his class. If the vast thousands of the Russian empire were not only taught to read, but inspired with a love of reading, and supplied with domestic libraries, who doubts that, in a few years, a miracle of national improvement would follow? Who doubts that every national aspect would be transformed, and the whole realm lifted up as by its four corners? The efficacy of such an experiment would be second only to that of a pure religious faith.

The *moral influence* of popular reading is invaluable. The maxim, that

"A little learning is a dangerous thing,"

may be true (though not without much qualification) when applied to the scientific and the would-be learned, but it is altogether fallacious in respect to popular intelligence. The people are not speculative; they are not generally vain; they are frank, confiding, implicit. Though the chief sufferers by religious or political errors, yet are they seldom their originators. They have too little presumption to disbelieve received truths, and too much common sense to propound theoretical absurdities; if they cannot be learned, still they may be intelligent without danger. Their intelligence is the conservative virtue of society. It is not the influence of the highly learned which preserves a community from the corruptions of error, but the aggregate intelligence of the middling classes. If religion is the salt of the earth, this is a part of its savor —it always coexists with genuine religion, and cannot exist without it.

Books are good means of *domestic enjoyment and virtue;* and if ever there comes a golden age of popular intelligence, its indication will be the *domestic library*, not scattered amid the rubbish of shelves, or concealed in the privacy of a closet, but placed prominently in the parlor as its most esteemed furniture. Next to the beautiful scene of domestic worship, what is more delightful than the sight of a family plying at the fireside the light tasks of the evening, listening to the voice of the reader, and varying the tranquil scene by conversational remarks? A love of books thus inspired in the minds of the young may have the most salutary influence on their coming years. It may develop the latent energies of genius, or quicken and attemper the aspirations of early virtue and piety. The mechanic, with such an attraction at his hearth, will learn to despise the gross pleasures of vice and conviviality; and the affluent and the educated will find in such a combination of the pleasures of the mind with the affections of the heart, one of the most elevated delights of life. A distinguished living writer gives an example in the history of the lamented *Princess Charlotte:*—" She and her consort, Prince Leopold, lived together in the greatest harmony and affection; and, from what her biographers have stated respecting her education and pursuits, it appears that the mutual friendship of these illustrious individuals was heightened and cemented by the rational conversation in which they indulged, and the elevated studies to which they were devoted. Her course of education embraced the English, classical, French, German, and Italian languages: arithmetic, geography, astronomy, the first six books of Euclid, algebra, mechanics, and the principles of optics and perspective, with history, the policy of governments, and particularly the principles of the Christian religion. She was also a skillful musician, had a fine conception of the picturesque in nature, and was fond of drawing. She took great pleasure in strolling on the beach, in marine excursions, in walking in the country, in rural scenery, in conversing freely with the rustic inhabitants, and in investigating every object which seemed worthy of her attention. She was an enthusiastic admirer of the grand and beautiful in nature, and the ocean was to her an object of peculiar interest. After her union with the prince, as their tastes were similar, they engaged in the same studies. Gardening, drawing, music, and rational conversation, diversified their leisure hours. They took great pleasure in the culture of flowers, in the classification of them, and in the formation, with scientific skill, of a *hortus siccus*. But the *library*, which was furnished with the best books in our language, was their favorite place of resort; and their chief daily pleasure was mutual instruction. They were seldom apart, either in their occupations or in their amusements; nor were they separated in their religious duties. 'They took sweet counsel together, and walked to the house of God in company;' and it is also stated, on good authority, that they maintained the worship of God in their family, which was regularly attended by every branch of their household. No wonder, then, that they exhibited an auspicious and a delightful example of private and domestic virtue, of *conjugal attachment*, and of unobtrusive charity and benevolence."

MIGHTY MEN.

"*We shall reap if we faint not.*"—St. Paul

The truly mighty men of history were made such more by industry than by genius. Let the lesson be well learned by the young. There have been great men who were not able men—fictitiously great; their greatness arising more from their fortunate circumstances than from themselves; but the truly great have generally been the "laboring classes" of their respective departments, genuine workmen. The young man who does not feel strongly within him the disposition to *work*, may entertain no high ambition for usefulness or eminence.

Dr. Samuel Clarke said the old adage of "too many irons in the fire conveys an abominable old lie; have all in, shovel, tongs, and poker." It is not so much the multiplicity of employments, as the want of system in them, that disturbs and injures both the work and workman. Wesley did everything by system, and how much did he achieve? He traveled about five thousand miles a year, preached about three times a day, beginning at five o'clock in the morning, and his published works amount to about two hundred volumes.

Asbury traveled about six thousand miles a year, and preached incessantly. Coke crossed the Atlantic eighteen times, preached, wrote, traveled, established missions, begged from door to door for them, and labored in all respects as if, like the apostles, he would "turn the world upside down." At nearly seventy years of age he started to Christianize India! Baxter, with numerous and grievous diseases, wrote a surprising number of books, practiced physic, and, as he took no fees, was oppressed with patients; spent two days a week in cate-chetical instruction, and, besides special sermons and several regular evening services, preached three times a week. Calvin, tortured with gout, stranguary, stone, catarrh, and other infirmities, acted, while in Geneva, as pastor and professor, wrote nine folio volumes, with profound thought, corresponded with all parts of the continent, every other day lectured, and every other week preached daily. He states, in one of his letters, the work of one day while at Strasburgh. It consists of a sermon, a lecture, the correction of twenty sheets of manuscript, four letters, besides offices of advice and reconciliation in more than a dozen cases. Luther was one of the most extensive writers of his age. He maintained an immense correspondence, the published part filling numerous volumes, lectured regularly before the university, preached nearly every day, bore the chief burden of the churches, fought emperor, pope, and council, lived constantly in the agitation of controversy, and yet found leisure for the enjoyments of domestic life, and the recreations of music and poety. Nearly all these wonderful men were always oppressed with poverty. Wesley left not more than ten pounds for his funeral expenses; Asbury received not two dollars a week, besides his entertainment and traveling expenses; Baxter received sixty pounds a year; Calvin sold his books to pay his rent; and Luther had to beg a coat of the elector.

"Labor conquers all things," was a maxim worthy of the nation which conquered the world. It is the testimony of almost all literary biography, that intellectual greatness is most commonly found, at first, in obscurity and poverty. In the higher walks of life, where the pleasures and honors of opulence pamper the sensuality and flatter the vanity of the mind, it is seldom capable of those high aspirations which lead to intellectual eminence—while in poverty and obscurity it is dependent upon its own resources. It must remain unhonored, or rise by the might of its own energy. It acquires in such circumstances one quality, at 'east, which lies at the foundation of all true greatness of mind, *a noble sense of self-dependence.*

Nearly all the great names, conspicuous on the catalogue of renown, are proofs of the success of mind in contending with difficulties.

Metastasios, a friendless lad, singing verses in the streets, became one of the greatest authors in Italian literature. Gifford, the cabin boy, was one of the most powerful writers of his age. Epictetus, the moralist, was born a slave, but became the boast of the stoical sect of philosophers, and the intimate friend of the best emperors of Rome. Ferguson was a shepherd's boy, but raised himself to the honor of the first astronomer of his age, at whose lectures royalty itself listened with delight. Murray was a shepherd's boy, but he became one of the first instructors of mankind. Brown, the author of the Commentary, Concordance, and Bible Dictionary, was likewise a shepherd's boy. Terence was an African slave, but raised himself to such an elevation that the haughty consuls of Rome courted his society. Franklin, the printer, became one of the first men of his age. Sir Humphrey Davy, the son of a woodcarver, and the apprentice of an apothecary, became the first chemist of his times. Columbus, the sailor, left a new world for his memorial. Roger Sherman, the statesman of the American Revolution, was a shoemaker. Herschel, the great astronomer, was a British soldier in Nova Scotia; he commenced the study of astronomy while watching on the sentry post at night, and has fixed his name among the orbs. Samuel Lee was a carpenter, but became a professor of Hebrew in Cambridge University, England. Adam Clarke was the son of a country schoolmaster, but rose to be one of the first Biblical scholars of modern times. Robert Hall was the son of a poor dissenting minister; he became one of the most splendid orators of the British pulpit, and one of the best writers of the English language. Cuvier, the greatest of modern naturalists, was the son of a pensioned soldier, and a charity scholar at college. Prideaux, the author of the "Connections," and bishop of Worcester, could not be kept at school by his poor parents longer than to learn to read and write, and he obtained the rest of his education by walking to Oxford and obtaining employment in the kitchen of Exeter College.

Nearly the whole list of worthies on the record of literary fame were thus diamonds found in the mine—pearls brought up from the depths of obscurity—men who, but for their own energy, would have passed away, with the mass of mankind, "little and unknown."

The most essential requisite for the pursuit of knowledge, under such circumstances, is *unyielding determination.* This is of such great importance, as almost to make up for deficiency in any other respect. It is truly wonderful what this noble quality has accomplished. The history of literature is full of its miracles. In cases where ordinary intellects would quail in despair, minds nerved with this high energy of purpose have seemed only to gather new strength, have wrought themselves into a kind of omnipotency which has swept away the most appalling difficulties, and enabled them to trample into the dust the most formidable obstacles. It is, even in many cases, preferable to genius. Genius is morbid, erratic, burning too often in fitful gleams, or with too intense ardor, so as to consume itself. It is brilliant like a meteor, but has no fixed laws to keep it steady. Genius frequently leads to disregard of the means of improvement, and thereby disappoints its own hopes. But an ordinary mind, strengthened with this lofty resolve, is regular in its progress; it may be slow, but it is sure. It does not rush onward, breathless and wild, like a frantic maniac but moves with majestic calmness, stepping always on a sure position, and surveying the way as it goes. Genius is fit for extra circumstances only; a determined though ordinary mind is common place. It is practical, and can handle common things. Genius is like the precious gold ore, which is adapted to shine, a pretty thing, an ornament for the finger or ear, or fit for the nice workmanship of a watch; a common mind nerved with resolution is like the ruder but more useful ore of iron, fit alike for a steam engine, an artillery piece to hurl its blazing thunder, or a gleaming sword. Genius is a fragile flower which blossoms beautifully and fades easily; a practical but determined mind can grow up in the storm, like the oak, spread its limbs to battle with the winds, and though it may be shorn of its "leafy honors" by the wintry blast, yet its roots are deep in the earth, its branches strong, and when the summer returns it thrives as vigorously as ever.

I have met somewhere with a noble passage on the subject; it is evidently the opinion of a master mind: "More is to be expected from laborious mediocrity than from the erratic efforts of a wayward genius. Demosthenes elaborated sentence after sentence, and Newton rose to the heavens by the steps of geometry, and said, at the close of his career, that it was only in the habit of patient thinking he was conscious of differing from other men. It is generally thought that men are signalized more by talent than by industry; it is felt to be a vulgarizing of genius to attribute it to anything but direct inspiration from Heaven; they overlook the steady and persevering devotion of mind to one subject. There are higher and lower walks in scholarship, but the highest is a walk of labor. We are often led into a contrary opinion by looking at the magnitude of the object in its finished state, such as the 'Principia' of Newton, and the Pyramids of Egypt, without reflecting on the gradual, continuous, I had almost said, creeping progress by which they grew into objects of the greatest magnificence in the literary and physical world. In the one case, indeed, we may fancy the chisel which wrought each successive stone, but in the other we cannot trace the process by which the philosopher was raised from one landing-place to another, till he soared to his towering elevation; it seems as if the work was produced at the bidding of a magician. But Newton has left, as a legacy, the assurance, that he did not attain his elevation by a heaven-born inspiration, out of the reach of many, but by dint of a homely virtue within the reach of all."

Reader, art thou a young man struggling against difficulties for improvement and usefulness? Hold up then bravely thy head, when the surge rolls over thee. Knowest thou not that the energy which works within thee is the measure of thy capability; that whatsoever thou willest thou canst achieve, if not interdicted by the laws of thy being? Look, then, on obstacles with an unblinking eye. Most of the good and the great of all ages have been thy fellows in suffering, and thou mayest be theirs in success. Despond not; good counselors will tell thee to be humble; their counsel is wise; but remember humility is not a fiction; it is the right estimate of thyself, not depreciation. Humility is strength. She is brave. She has lifted many a time her meek eye serenely in the flames of the stake. Be humble, then, but be strong in thy heart. Thy soul is an exhaustless energy, the wide world is open for thine action, and voices from earth and heaven summon thee to dare and to do.

JACK AND HIS MASTER.

" Bless them that curse you."—Christ.

Two of these sketches have already related to the influence of religion on the negro character. Many more might be given. It has been no small happiness of my ministerial life to preach often to these lowly children of Ham. I have found among them some of the best disciples of my Master—"living epistles." Whatever may be the defects of the African mind, it is not deficient in the moral and social affections. Religion takes profound hold of it, and enlivens it with a spiritual vivacity which I have often seen spreading the smiles of gladness over its most abject depressions.

Though constitutionally timid, I have known them to endure "fiery trials" for Christ with a meek fortitude which has subdued the violence of persecution. I have somewhere met with an affecting instance, but cannot recall its source or authority, and cannot, therefore, vouch for its truth; but it is so characteristic and so accordant with my knowledge of the negro heart when influenced by the love of Christ, as to give it strong probability. It is the case of a slave who became a local preacher, and in one of his sermons relates the story as follows:—

"When I was a lad there were no religious people near where I lived. But I had a young master about my age, who was going to school, and he was very fond of me. At night he would come into the kitchen to teach me the lesson he had learned himself during the day at school. In this way I learned to read.

"When I was well nigh grown up, we took up the New Testament, and agreed to read it verse by verse. When one would make a mistake the other was to correct him, so that we could learn to read well.

"In a short time we both felt that we were sinners before God, and we both agreed to seek the salvation of our souls. The Lord heard our prayer, and gave us both a hope in Christ. Then I began to hold meetings for prayer and exhortation among the colored people.

"My old master soon found out what was going on. He was very angry, especially because his son had become pious. He forbid my holding any more meetings, saying, that if I did, he would whip me severely for it.

"From that time I continued to preach or exhort on sabbaths and sabbath nights; and on Monday morning my old master would tie me up, and cut my back to pieces with a cowhide, so that it had never time to get well. I was obliged to do my work in a great deal of pain from day to day.

"Thus I lived near a year and a half. One Monday morning my master, as usual, had made my fellow-slaves tie me to a shade-tree in the yard, after stripping my back naked to receive the cowhide. It was a beautiful morning in the summer time, and the sun shone very bright. Everything around looked very pleasant. He came up to me with cool deliberation, took his stand, and looked at me closely, but the cowhide hung still at his side. His conscience was at work, and it was a great moment in his life.

" 'Well Jack,' said he, 'your back is covered all over with scars and sores, and I see no place to begin to whip. You obstinate wretch, how long do you intend to go on in this way?'

" 'Why, master, just as long as the Lord will let me live,' was my reply.

" 'Well, what is your design in it?'

" 'Why, master, in the morning of the resurrection, when my poor body shall rise from the grave, I intend to show these scars to my heavenly Father, as so many witnesses of my faithfulness in his cause.'

"He ordered them to untie me, and sent me to hoe corn in the field. Late in the evening he came along, pulling a weed here, and a weed there, till he got to me, and then told me to sit down.

"'Jack,' said he, 'I want you to tell me the truth. You know that for a long time your back has been sore from the cowhide; you have had to work very hard, and are a poor slave. Now tell me, are you happy or not, under such troubles as these?'

"'Yes, master, I believe I am as happy a man as there is on earth.'

"'Well, Jack,' said he, 'I am not happy. Religion, you say, teaches you to pray for those that injure you. Now, will you pray for your old master, Jack?'

"'Yes; with all my heart,' said I.

"We kneeled down, and I prayed for him. He came again and again to me. I prayed for him in the field, till he found peace in the blood of the Lamb. After this we lived together like brothers in the same church. On his death-bed he gave me my liberty, and told me to go on preaching as long as I lived, and meet him at last in heaven.

"I have seen," said Jack, "many Christians whom I loved, but I have never seen any I loved so well as my old master. I hope I shall meet him in heaven."

RELIGIOUS CHEERFULNESS.

"*Always rejoicing.*"—Paul.

It is one of those commands which may be considered as more recommendatory than imperative, when the apostle says, "*Rejoice evermore.*" Yet no one can doubt that not only the general spirit, but the express letter, of the gospel favors a happy and even joyful temper. No one who reads the Scriptures with a direct reference to this point can be unconscious of the fact that while they may not unqualifiedly condemn dejection, they nevertheless discountenance it, as not only foreign to religion, but generally hostile to it. How infatuated, then, the impression of many, especially among the young, that spiritual-mindedness is essentially sombre!

Look for a moment at the *spirit* of true religion. Gloom and severity of mind usually associate with misanthropy; but the central element of religion is *love*—love intense, supreme, ever-growing. Remorse is a painful source of mental misery; yet it is chiefly by the absence of *hope* that the mind languishes. What a terrible word is *despair:* yet its most fearful import is *hopelessness.* But how full of fruition is the future to a Christian mind—endless, boundless fruition! Repose your thoughts a moment on the strong language of the Scriptures: "A good hope," "a lively hope," "a blessed hope," "rejoicing in hope," "abounding in hope," "full assurance of hope." Choose any other attribute essential to the mental frame of the Christian, and you will find it in contrast with gloom; as much so as the star is with the darkness in which it shines.

Assuredly there can be found nothing in the *practical system* of Christianity which is repugnant to a happy temper. How pure are its ordinances; how simple and tranquil its worship; how befitting, and coincident with our daily cares, its duties! Christianity is indeed a *discipline*; it imposes self-denial. It has its "burden," but its burden is "light;" it has its "yoke," but its yoke is "easy."

What, then, are the causes of the not unfrequent depression met with among Christians?

It may be remarked in reply, first, that physical causes often contribute to it. Let not this be deemed an unimportant observation. We are not assured that it is not the chief cause of mental sufferings among those who are genuine Christians. It should be borne in mind that a conformity to the moral laws of our being does not supersede obedience to the physical and organic laws: and that while we reap the rewards of obedience in the one case, we may be suffering the penalties of transgression in the other. The Christian should aim at perfection in all respects. Some of our strongest temptations are connected with physical circumstances. We should therefore include our bodily health among our moral duties.

Again: no doubt much of the depression of the Christian arises from the remains of sin. Every drop of gall has its bitterness. The only resource here is, to seize St. Paul's remedy, "*Go on to perfection.*" Holiness is essential to happiness. There never was a truer and loftier maxim. Even what you may consider small sins, must ever interfere, while they are indulged, with your peace. Needles can pierce deeper than larger instruments. A secret sin is often more injurious to the soul than an overt or gross crime. It has a character of concealment, of hypocrisy, that makes it more degrading. Are you habitually or occasionally unhappy, Christian reader? Look now deliberately into your heart, and see if the cause is not obvious. Perhaps the greatest curse your heavenly Father could inflict upon you would be a happy frame of mind, while you are omitting, it may be forgetting, his command that you "be perfect, even as he is perfect." How amazing is the undoubted fact, that many Christians shrink from this command, because they fear that the higher responsibility and minuter fidelity of a sanctified state will form a servitude in which they will be unhappy! Young Christian, bethink you! Is such a fancy found on the page of God's word? Is the shadowy twilight more brilliant than the full glory of the day? How superlatively wretched heaven must be, if you are correct! Christian perfection is indeed a high state, and its watchfulness and fidelity are correspondently great; but it is a state of extraordinary *grace*, as well as of extraordinary *duty*. It is perfect *love* that "*casts out fear*." Is it not, then, on the mere score of enjoyment, preferable to an inferior degree of piety? Would you be *glad* with joy? Would you triumph over care and anxiety, and sin and death; and, above all, over yourself and the devil? Would you have the perfection of all the happiness to be enjoyed in this world? Abandon sin. Fly from sin. Abhor it; shudder at it. Look upon its smallest stain as upon a plague spot.

Again. Are not we Christians wondrously thoughtless? Do we not walk amidst the outstanding, the blazing glories of our blessed region, like the blind man beneath the starry grandeur of the firmament, or amid the effulgence of the sun? Does not the want of a *meditative habit* lead to that vacancy and cheerlessness of mind which we often feel? When we open God's word in an hour of gloom, it ought to be to us like a sun outbursting from the heaven in midnight. How full of clear counsel, and happy words, and radiant doctrine, and sweet assurance, and bounding hope, is it! O, it is indeed the *gospel*—good and glad tidings. How every passage dilates and palpitates with unutterable mercy and love! " Glory in the highest," shouted the angels when they announced it over Bethlehem; and so should we respond, whenever we look at it.

Young Christian, try to *think* as well as to *feel*. What mind, not absolutely in a state of fatuity, can habitually meditate upon the great topics of revealed religion, and be miserable and driveling? Select any one of its essential doctrines, and you have what might be the text of an angel's study, and that study protracted through eternity. What a conception is the character of its God! What a topic the atonement! How full of confidence and assurance the truth of a special providence! How relieving and consoling the fact of justification by faith! How sublime the resurrection! and how all-glorious the truth of "immortality and eternal life!" Christian, if the gospel is true, God, even God, loves *you!* His Son died for *you;* angels guard *you;* devils quail before *you;* death drops his sceptre at *your* approach; the grave fades away at *your* feet; time will grow oblivious, and worlds waste into nothingness, while *you* but pass through your intellectual infancy! Lift up your hands, then, and bless the God and Father of our Lord Jesus Christ. Disdain your trivial trials, and blush to think that the possessor of all these "riches of glory" should have ever hung his head a moment in despondence.

TOO LATE.

" He that being often reproved, hardeneth his neck, shall suddenly be destroyed, and that without remedy."
                                                    Solomon.

ONE of the most remarkable outpourings of the Spirit of God I ever witnessed was at a quarterly meeting in L——. In those days, and especially in that wilderness region, quarterly meetings were the high festivals of the church. They continued at least two days, the people assembled for many miles around, and most of the neighboring farm-houses were thrown open for the hospitable entertainment of the throng.

The services commenced early on Saturday morning, and continued without intermission, except for sleep at night, till ten o'clock Sunday evening. The venerable father O. preached the first sermon with resistless power. The windows of heaven were opened, and a blessing poured out, such as we could not contain: the crowded house, and the throngs outside, about the doors and windows, seemed spell-bound. Sinners trembled and wept, and the people of God shouted for joy. During all that day and the next, prayer meetings and love-feasts occupied the intervals of the sermons, and while one portion of the laborers went to their meals or reposed themselves, another supplied their places. Thirty-four persons professed to have passed from death unto life during the two days, and many others were awakened. My heart kindles afresh as I think of that blessed occasion. There is but one melancholy recollection connected with it, which I record for the warning of others.

Mr. G., a pious and laborious local preacher, came with his wife, son, and two daughters, more than ten miles, to that meeting, with particular reference to the salvation of his son, who had been the subject of his paternal prayers for more than eighteen years, and was the only one of his family that remained unsaved. During these years he had often been deeply convicted of sin, but resistance had become habitual, and the aged parent was fearful that the habit would become confirmed and fatal. It deeply affects me even now to recall the tears and prayers of the good old man in behalf of his son during the meeting. While others rejoiced at the penitent throngs that pressed around the altar for prayers, he wept for the child of his love who appeared not among them.

There is sometimes danger of too much importunity in personal conversations on religion with our impenitent friends. Such is the natural perversity of the human heart, that unless we are cautious our appeals will only throw them into an attitude of self-defense, a studied resistance of religious impressions—a habit most hardening to the heart. The anxious father was fully aware of this danger: during the meeting he was affectionately earnest, but not too frequent in his conversations with the young man. He prayed incessantly for him, and trusted to the influence of the public means of grace. One exercise after another passed, but with no visible effect on his mind. The sabbath afternoon had arrived, and scores were weeping at the altar, when the anxious parent came to request me to seek out his child and faithfully converse with him.

I found him, urged him to immediate repentance, and recommended him to place himself among the mourning group at the altar.

"The Scriptures do not require me to go to the altar," he answered, "and can I not receive religion elsewhere as well as there?"

"Yes," I replied, "the Lord can save you where you now stand, or anywhere else, if you earnestly seek him, but what place can be more appropriate for those who earnestly seek him than the altar of his sanctuary? We baptize our children there; there we receive candidates into his church, and perform the solemnities of marriage, and the obsequies of the dead; it is a holy place, and why is it not appropriate that our first religious vows should be taken there? There is, indeed, no special virtue in the altar, but by going to it you will place yourself in a position to receive more directly the prayers and counsels of God's people. You will also thereby own yourself on the Lord's side, and break at once that dangerous diffidence which has ruined thousands. I do not say that you cannot obtain religion without going to the altar, but I do say that you will never obtain it until you overcome those feelings which prevent your going: you can never obtain it till you are sufficiently humbled to receive it anywhere, or at any sacrifice."

I spent half an hour in reasoning with him. He treated me with great respect, acknowledged his necessity of religion, but suggested a thousand difficulties. I left him with the painful conviction that, amidst all the wonderful influences of the occasion, he had succeeded in keeping his conscience asleep.

The meeting closed on Sunday night. On Monday morning, as I passed to my next appointment, I found the road enlivened with the horses and vehicles of the returning multitude. After riding four miles, I perceived a throng about a farm-house before me. I rode rapidly to it, and learned that a young man had been thrown from his horse and dangerously injured. I passed through the crowd to the chamber where they had placed the sufferer, and found the young man whom I had warned so emphatically the day before. He was shockingly injured, and as I entered the room a thrill of dismay seemed to pass over him. A physician soon arrived and pronounced the case hopeless, and declared that he could not survive two hours. Never shall I forget the agonized countenance of the wretched youth when he learned his fate.

"Must I die?" he exclaimed: "Is there no hope? O I cannot die! I cannot die!" I endeavored to direct him to the cross, and reminded him of the crucified thief.

"Alas!" he replied, "he never sinned against such light as I have abused.. What shall I do? Pray for me, O pray for me!"

We knelt down about the chamber, but his agonizing groans struck all with horror and confusion. I rose, and endeavored again to direct him to the Lamb of God who taketh away the sins of the world.

"*It is too late!*" he exclaimed, "O what

would I not give if I had heeded your warning yesterday, but it is now too late; I am lost! I am lost!"

His parents and sisters soon arrived; but the scene which followed I will not and cannot describe. The groans of the poor sufferer ceased only with his life, which occurred during the morning. He seemed stunned by the sudden and unexpected summons, and unable to command his thoughts sufficiently to pray. Who can describe the feelings of that poor dying youth! Who can imagine them! His body in agony, his life reduced to a few hours, and no preparation for eternity!

Reader! be ye ready for in such an hour as ye think not the summons may come!

>"Reflect, thou hast a soul to save,
> Thy sins, how high they mount!
> What are thy hopes beyond the grave?
> How stands that dark account?

>"Death enters, and there's no defense;
> His time there's none can tell:
> He'll in a moment call thee hence,
> To heaven or down to hell!"

END OF VOL. I.

SKETCHES & INCIDENTS;

OR,

A BUDGET FROM THE SADDLE-BAGS

OF A

SUPERANNUATED ITINERANT

VOLUME II.

GEORGE PECK, EDITOR.

Cincinnati:
PUBLISHED BY A. POE & L. HITCHCOCK,
FOR THE METHODIST EPISCOPAL CHURCH, AT THE WESTERN BOOK
CONCERN, CORNER OF MAIN AND EIGHTH STREETS.

R. P. THOMPSON, PRINTER.
1853.

Entered, according to Act of Congress, in the year 1845 by G. LANE & C. B. TIPPETT, in the Clerk's Office of the District Court of the Southern District of New-York.

PREFACE.

In preparing these pages the writer has contemplated two designs: first, the preservation of some of the more interesting of those denominational incidents which are current in our church, and which strikingly illustrate the providence of God; and secondly, the production of a work adapted to the advanced youth of the church—a department of our denominational literature hitherto almost entirely vacant. During some years he has had an eye on these objects; and, as in hours of leisure or indisposition, he penned one after another of these fragments, they were placed in his old saddle-bags: one budget has already been taken thence and given to the public. Its reception has encouraged the appearance of another.

Some of these articles present coincidences and *denouements* so remarkable as to probably excite suspicion of their veracity. The reader will bear in mind that such singular incidents do occasionally occur in the current of common-place events—that the present examples are not given as specimens of average events, but are professedly sought out as anomalous. Though the writer has discreetly (as he thinks) used his imagination, in a few instances, for the illustration of important subjects, yet most of the extraordinary cases referred to, so far as they are related on his own authority, he knows to be substantial facts; and those related on the authority of others are well authenticated.

CONTENTS.

	Page
The Love-feast	7
Literary and Moral Aspects of England at the Birth of Methodism	27
Bishop Asbury and Black Punch	43
A Theological Sketch	52
Mother Suma and the Wealthy Convert	65
Doctrinal Character of Methodism	74
The Praying Mother	83
The Jews	90
An Incident with a Lesson	96
Special Character of Methodism	101
Visit to the Tomb of Whitefield	119
Christian Use of Money	130
Bishop Roberts	143
Heretical Tendencies of Methodism and Calvinism	156
Wesleyan Anecdotes	161
A Meditative Habit	171
The Mariner's Preacher	176
The Sabbath School	183

SKETCHES AND INCIDENTS

THE LOVE-FEAST.

"Then they that feared the Lord spake often one to another."—Malachi.

The old quarterly conferences and love-feasts! what was more characteristic of practical Methodism than they? The horses and carriages, and groups of men, women, and children plodding the highways on foot, for twenty miles, or more, as on a holy pilgrimage; the assemblage of preachers, traveling and local, from all the neighboring appointments; the two days of preaching and exhorting, praying and praising; the powerful convictions, and more powerful conversions; and especially the Sunday morning love-feast, with its stirring testimonies and kindling songs; its tears and shoutings—how precious their reminiscences! Alas, for the changes which are coming over us!

An accurate description of one of these occasions would be among the best pictures of primitive Methodism. Shall I attempt to draw, not to paint, one which took place, not in the earliest times, yet at a period when the first generation of Methodists, ripe in their Christian experience, still lingered among us?

It was held in ——, a rural neighborhood. The locality was favorable for the assemblage of very various characters; and a more diversified company I have seldom met than were brought together at that quarterly love-feast.

It was a bright June morning; the adjacent fields were fragrant with the fresh hay; the orchards were vocal with the melody of birds; long lines of horses and Jersey wagons, interspersed with an occasional chaise, or carriage, of higher pretension, ranged along either side of the road, while saddle horses crowded the shady retreat of a neighboring forest. The church was an old frame structure, unpainted inside or out, but thoroughly neat and clean, and looking, on that warm day, with all its sashes out, most comfortably cool and airy. No dull blinds darkened the windows, and threw, as in city churches, a sepulchral gloom over the worshipers; but long, snow-white, cotton curtains flapped in the breezy air, as if playfully willing to admit an occasional gleam of sunlight, provided it would treat respectfully the eyes of the multitude. The pulpit (a high, narrow box, in the old style) and the altar were crowded with preachers, itinerant and local. The front gallery was filled with blacks, mostly slaves.

When I looked around at the large throng, fanned by the soft breezes, I expected soon to see many nodding, and feared a languid meeting; but, as they were singing, to the tune of China, the introductory hymn, a visible emotion spread through the assembly. Some tears flowed during the second verse,—

> "Still let us own our common Lord,
> And bear his easy yoke;
> A band of love, a threefold cord,
> Which never can be broke."

The feeling deepened as the long but beautiful hymn advanced; at last, as they closed the eighth stanza,—

> "With ease our souls through death shall glide
> Into their paradise;
> And thence, on wings of angels, ride
> Triumphant through the skies,"—

old brother B., who, by the way, was a famous shouter, could control himself no longer, but exclaimed, in a tone fraught with his whole soul, "Amen! glory be to God!" It thrilled the assembly, and sobs and ejaculations were

heard over the whole congregation. A powerful
prayer, by the presiding elder, followed, mingled with the fervent importunities of the congregation, during which my own soul was so
subdued that I wept like a child, and felt as if
I were bowing right under a cloud of the "excellent glory." Ah! fellow-Christian, have you
never felt thus borne, by the tide of prevailing
supplication, quite up to the gate of heaven?
Have you never felt as if you were kneeling,
with bowed head, on the very door-step of the
celestial temple, wetting it with tears, amid
the beatific vision, like the penitent, bowing at
the portal of the ancient church, but forbidden
to enter?

A stirring hymn followed:—

"Salvation! O the joyful sound!
What pleasure to our ears!
A sovereign balm for every wound,
A cordial for our fears;"

and then commenced the speaking. The venerable presiding elder, a tall, erect figure, with
white hair combed behind his ears, and countenance weather-worn, but full of sensibility,
after a few general remarks, referred, with
emotions that often interrupted his utterance,
to his own long experience. "I have been

traveling heavenward, blessed be God, nearly thirty years, and the road grows brighter as I approach the light of the better world. More than twenty-nine years ago, brother Freeborn Garrettson, who used to sound the trumpet through all these regions, came into the neighborhood of my father's plantation. One of my father's black servants, old Marcus, now in heaven, I have no doubt, [a loud shout from brother B.,] had wandered away some miles to the preaching and been soundly converted to God. The change was so remarkable that my good old father, who was trying to get to heaven as well as he knew how, invited brother Garrettson to preach in our vicinity. He arrived one day at noon, and Marcus and I spent all the afternoon in riding among the plantations, inviting the neighbors to hear him. In the evening he preached in our large kitchen. It was filled with attentive hearers, white and black. During the first prayer, when the preacher prayed for the family, and especially for the children, I felt a strange influence come into my soul. Old Marcus, who knelt near me, responded fervently to the prayer. He was weeping, and I heard him repeatedly breathe my name in his supplications. I felt then as I never had before The preacher took his text, and preached with power from on high; truth after truth flashed on my spirit like lightnings from heaven; the people wept all around me; but I could not; yet I trembled from head to foot. I seized the back of Marcus's seat to steady myself. I heard him breathe, ' Lord, save young massa.' My knees began to smite the one against the other. I hastened out of the door into the yard, and flew to a hay-stack, where I fell to the earth, crying for mercy. Soon one was praying by my side. It was old Marcus. He had seen my agitation, and followed me to the place. The scene that ensued I cannot describe. The poor negro prayed with me half the night, when the light broke from heaven upon my trembling soul, and then we wept together for joy. My old father soon after found the peace he had long been seeking, and my dear old mother followed in his steps. Father, mother, and black Marcus, have all gone home in triumph, and I feel this morning that I am not far from the 'heavenly Jerusalem,' 'the city of the living God.' I am old and gray; I can only totter on the way; my old fellow-laborers are mostly gone. A few, as Cooper, Garrettson, Ware, Dunwody, and others, linger still; but a new generation has come upon the stage; we can but now and then find one that belonged to our day. We are become not only as 'pilgrims,' but as 'strangers' among you, in the flesh, though not in the spirit. But now we 'desire a better country.'" The old man's utterance was choked by his emotions, and he sat down as they sung, with manifest feeling, the beautiful stanza,—

> "We are traveling home to God,
> In the way our fathers trod;
> They are happy now, and we
> Soon their happiness shall see."

Some eight or ten followed in rapid succession, all bearing good, though not remarkable, testimonies. I noticed, from the time the presiding elder had mentioned the name of Marcus, a deep sensation among the blacks who crowded the gallery. At this stage of the meeting one of them, an old, bald-headed, labor-worn man, unable apparently to restrain his feelings longer, rose, and addressing himself to the presiding elder, said, as the big tears ran freely, "Ah! massa, me neber forget old Marcus, bless de Lord! He lead me to massa Jesus. He come ober one night to our quarters and preached, and de Lord send down someting dat gat into me and shook me like an old torn handkerchief in de gale, bless de Lord! [Loud amens.] Me cried out for mercy, and Marcus cried wid me, and de Lord heard us, glory to his name! and when de morning come me felt, bless de Lord! like flying right up into de sun. De Lord has been berry good to me since den; he feed me ebery day wid de manna from heaven, bless his name! My poor Nancy he save too; she suffered much tree weeks in dreadful pain; but she did'nt complain a word, but said de Lord was doing all right. She went up wid her hand on de head of little Neddy, blessing de child. Ah! dat night my heart like to break! but de quarters seemed full of light; none of us slept, but prayed all night.

"And poor Neddy has gone up since den too, praising de Lord all de way till he could'nt be heard, bless de Lord! And now me waiting, brodders, to go; me old and weary, but journeying onward; O bless de Lord! me feel dis morning like going right up."

Loud exclamations and many tears followed, especially among the blacks. These poor creatures included many of the best Christians I have ever known, though no little extravagance sometimes attended their devotions; and among them also were found instances of deception and hypocrisy. Imbecility, moral as well as mental, is almost inseparable from their servile condition, and renders their religion often very doubtful. An example occurred at this time. One of the slaves spoke most rapturously. He belonged to a local preacher, who was present, and who had lately missed many of his poultry. His master had reason to suspect that he had taken them at night and cooked them in his quarters. After the love-feast I heard the master speaking to the servant, who seemed yet under the excitement of the meeting:—" Well, Sammy, what about the lost chickens, eh? Do you know anything about them, Sammy?"

" O no, massa, bless de Lord! me be honest; me know nothing about de chickens, massa."

As I was passing to a neighboring house. Sammy and his wife were walking before me. I overheard him saying, " But Molly, 'spose massa had axed me about de ducks instead of de chickens? den me been in a bad fix, eh, Molly? Jim took de chickens, but me only de ducks." I state it as an example of ingenious evasion, combined with weakness of moral perception—a characteristic not uncommon among slaves, and calling for careful instruction on the part of those who have the Christian charge of them.

But there are among them gems of Christian character, though set in ebony. Such a one arose after the last described. She was not old, yet broken down with sorrows, and apparently so feeble with pulmonary consumption as to be hardly able to speak loud enough to be heard through the house. A breathless silence was maintained while she spoke, as if all sympathized with her feebleness and grief. This poor creature had formerly belonged to a hardhearted planter, who had sold her husband and only child—the former was at this time in Louisiana, the latter in Alabama. The separation had broken her heart, and she was hastening to the grave under the pressure of insupportable wo. She had lately been converted. This change, though it could not arrest her fate, spread the brightness of hope over it. With a manner that betokened superior intelligence for her lot, and in tones of melting pathos, she said, " My heart-strings are broken, but God comforts me ; all that is dearest to me on earth has been torn from me, but my Saviour remains. I shall be here but a short time, but it is enough, since I have learned that this world is only a vale of tears, and that there is another ' where the wicked cease from troubling.' O! is there one here whose lot is one of grief and tears ? let a fellow-sufferer tell such that the Lord is a very present help in trouble. Though I stand here ruined in health and in my hopes of this life, yet is my soul steadfast in the Lord, and quiet in the hope of the relief which he will soon send me."

The assembly, which felt deeply for the sufferer, and, in common with most Christian planters, detested the slave-trade, then sung,—

"O what are all my suff'rings here,
  If, Lord, thou count me meet
With that enraptured host t' appear,
  And worship at thy feet!

"Give joy or grief, give ease or pain,
  Take life or friends away,
But let me find them all again
  In that eternal day!"

The example of this devoted slave opened the way for the white females. Among many that spoke, one said, "I thank God for a praying mother. I am one of four daughters who from infancy had the precious blessing of a mother's daily supplications. Years passed away without any visible change in any of us; but God only knows what deep exercises of mind I had during those years of apparent carelessness. My dear mother was once suddenly and dangerously seized with illness. Near the midhour of the night we were called to witness her departure, and receive her last blessing. O that dreary, yet blessed night, its remembrance can never fade! My dear parent was in agonizing pain, yet she could only think and pray for her children. Brother P., our beloved preacher, had arrived, and sat by her bedside 'Is the prospect of heaven bright, sister?' he asked. 'O yes,' she responded, 'heaven is bright, but earth is shaded in gloom to me. My poor children, must I leave them without God and without hope in the world! It seems impossible for me to die till I have witnessed their salvation, and can carry with me to the grave the hope of meeting them in heaven.'

"At these words, one of my sisters, who had been weeping profusely, threw herself at the bedside, exclaiming, 'Mother, if God will hear prayer, you shall not die without the hope of meeting me again.' I could sustain myself no longer, but fell on my knees at her side, and in a moment we were all four prostrate in prayer and tears. Brother P. knelt with us, and when morning dawned we were all humbly hoping in our Redeemer. My dear mother was so relieved by the change, that she recovered, and for years led us as Christiana, in Bunyan's Progress, did her children, in the pathway to heaven. She has since entered into her rest, and her daughters are this morning still on the way to meet her."

Brother B. here shouted aloud, accompanied by many others. When the emotion had subsided brother C., a traveling preacher, arose. "Brethren and sisters," said he, "many of you speak of the prayers of parents; I had no such blessing before my conversion, but I thank God that I can trust I have a parent in heaven, in answer to my own unworthy prayers. When quite young, I wandered away from my home in New-Jersey, to seek adventures in Ohio, then a howling wilderness. There, blessed be God, I found that Methodist itinerants had gone before me. They used to travel on the trail of the Indians, ford the streams, sleep under the trees with their saddle-bags for pillows, and preach day and night. I went to hear them once, and, though a desperate sinner, the word reached my heart. I cried out for mercy. Several weeks did I weep before the Lord, till at last I passed from death unto life, old things passed away, and behold all things became new.

"My thoughts turned immediately to my old father in New-Jersey. I prayed for him incessantly; but this could not satisfy me. I felt that I must go to him, tell him what the Lord had done for me, and exhort him to flee from the wrath to come. I started for New-Jersey, traveling on foot, and in such baggage-wagons as I found on the way. When I reached home my father was glad to see me, but laughed at my errand. He was skeptical, and thought me crazy. I stayed some time with him, but thought he heeded not my warnings. I perceived that he even began to grow vexed with my importunity. The devil tempted me to believe that I had been deluded by my feelings into fanatical folly. But I continued my efforts. I had fixed upon a time for my return to Ohio. The last day came, and yet my aged father remained unaffected. I determined to spend the last night in prayer for him in the barn. I felt that I would test God's promises to answer prayer that night. In an agony of spirit I went to the barn, and prayed without ceasing till after midnight. Suddenly I heard a cry outside. I listened; it was the voice of my sister: 'John,' said she, 'for mercy's sake, come to the house; father is crazy!'

"I ran to the house, flew up to my father's chamber, and found the old man on his knees, praying aloud and weeping like a child. Glory to God—my prayers had been heard! I delayed a day longer, and left my aged father on the way to heaven. He has entered into it since in triumph, and I expect soon to meet him there. The Lord has been good to me and mine; blessed be his holy name. Ye parents and children who are praying for each other, be not discouraged, for the promises of God are, in Christ Jesus, yea and amen."

A sailor here arose. "My friends," said he, "I have been tossed about the world several years, but could never forget my home here. When a boy, the Methodist preachers used to stay at my father's house. I remember many of them now, and shall always. When they rode up to the gate, I used to run out to take their horses to the stable; and then they would put their hands on my head and say, 'God bless you, Joseph; be a good boy, and pray the Lord to give you a new heart.' And how they would pray for me at family prayers! Nobody, perhaps, thought that these things would get much hold upon me; but, brothers, they were ringing in my ears all over the world, by day and by night, in calm and in storm. For years I resisted them, and became so dissipated that my poor mother died with no prospect of ever seeing me in heaven. I ran away and went to sea; and all thought there was little or no hope for me. But, though a terrible sinner, God never gave me up; those old Methodist preachers' faces and warnings followed me all over the

Atlantic, around Cape Horn, and in the Southern Ocean, giving me no rest, till one night I wandered into a prayer meeting, in a southern port, and began with tears and groans to call upon the Lord for mercy. Glory to his name, he received the prodigal, and I am come home here to see some old faces, and tell you what the Lord has done for me. Brethren, I am on board the heaven-bound ship, and am on the look-out for the harbor. I am very happy this morning, bless the Lord."

Here was sung,—

> "There all the ship's company meet,
>   Who sail'd with the Saviour beneath;
> With shouting each other they greet,
>   And triumph o'er sorrow and death:
>
> "The voyage of life's at an end,
>   The mortal affliction is past;
> The age that in heaven we spend,
>   For ever and ever shall last."

The singing started brother B. He rose with flowing tears, and exclaiming, "Glory be to God! I feel that I do not deserve to wash your feet; but I love *your* Redeemer, and he owns me this morning for his child, glory be to his name! He blessed me this morning, before daylight, while praying about this meeting, and my cup runs over. Hallelujah!" Brother B. was a man of few words, and no one did he use oftener than the term glory. As he said little, I must speak for him. Doubtless there was a trait of weakness in his nature; but such was the sincerity and purity of his character that the most fastidious admired him. He was privileged to shout, for it evidently came from his heart. I never knew a more devoted man. For twenty years I do not believe the sun found him in bed once: he anticipated the day in prayer and praise. At his family altar, especially in the evening, it was his custom, besides reading, singing, and prayer, to stand at his chair and give the family a warm exhortation; and the day was ended with his usual shouts of praise. Brother B., after shouting through twenty years, showed the ruling passion strong in death. He died shouting, enjoying what the dying Fletcher prayed for,—"a gust of praise."

I saw him three times in imminent danger, but he always at such times shouted. Once, when in a stage, the horses ran away on the verge of a dangerous precipice, he shouted for half a mile. "Glory to God, brother," said he, "we can go to heaven thus as well as in a chariot of fire."

Among many other interesting cases was that of a Dutchman. "Mine brodders," said he, "I have also mine story to tell about Gott's mercy. I was a great sinner, but I tot I was good enough. I tot it was enough to mind mine own business, and hear de parson once on a Sunday. All de rest of de Sunday I sat on de bench before mine door, drinking beer, smoaking mine pipe, and tinking about mine crops. But mine Shonny come home one day from one of de Metodist meetings, with his eyes all red, and said, 'O fader, we must come unto Christ, or we be all gone to ruin.' Shonny had been strange some days, and now, tot I, he is lost his senses. I called mine wife, and said, 'O wife, Shonny is ruined.' 'No, fader,' said he, 'I am seeking Gott's mercy, widout which we be all gone to ruin.' And den he talked at me one quarter hour wid tears, telling me about sin, hell, and de Saviour, Jesus Christ. When I went to mine bed dat night, mine eyes could not be shut; I tot only of dese tings. I tot wat goot would be all mine lands and cattles if I die and go into hell? De next morning I could not eat mine breakfast. I said to mine wife, she must send for de doctor. But I could not wait mine heart jumped, and I fell on mine knees and cried out, 'O, mine Gott, have mercy on me for I am going down into hell.' Shonny prayed wid me, and we prayed so every day, and we went to de Metodist meeting, and, glory be to God, he had mercy upon us, through our Saviour, Jesus Christ, and saved us from going down into hell. And now, mine brodders, I trust in mine Saviour, and try to get to heaven."

Such are specimens, interspersed among some fifty or more other testimonials, most of which came burning from the heart, and were responded to audibly by the joyous and yet weeping assembly. I have selected the most remarkable, but others were worthy of record, had I space for them. Some were strongly characteristic, some full of the marvelous, others despondingly humble. A few spoke of dark and mysterious workings of the mind, baffled with spiritual anxieties; others stood on Pisgah's top and saw

> "Sweet hills array'd in living green,
> And rivers of delight."

Some were rejoicing in the enjoyment of perfect love, others had just entered into spiritual life, and a few, trembling with penitential anguish, implored the prayers of the assembly. Rapturous songs varied the scene, most of them spirit-stirring stanzas from Charles Wesley, for the ditties of latter times had hardly begun to appear yet.

As I studied the scene before me I could not but admire the indications of character which it presented—the felicitous effect of religion on all varieties of temperament, and the remarkable operation of the energetic system of Methodism in seeking out and combining, in a common brotherhood, such diversified elements.

The meeting closed by singing the beautiful and appropriate hymn,—

> "Blest be the tie that binds
> Our hearts in Christian love;
> The fellowship of kindred minds
> Is like to that above."

LITERARY AND MORAL ASPECTS OF ENGLAND AT THE BIRTH OF METHODISM.

"*Perilous times.*"—Paul.

The circumstances which mark the origin of Methodism are no less interesting than those which distinguish its subsequent periods—they are in striking contrast with the latter, and must be considered in any just estimate of the singular success which has attended the development of the system.

The literature of the eighteenth century, particularly of its earlier part, is an important index to the moral character of that period. It presents a brilliant catalogue of names, among which are Addison, Steele, Berkeley, Swift, Pope, Congreve, Gray, Parnell, Young, Thomson, Rowe, Goldsmith, and Johnson, besides a splendid array in the more profound departments of knowledge. The intelligent reader may easily conjecture what must have been the moral aspects of English society when the loose wit of Congreve was the attraction of the British theatre, and, as Dryden declared, "the only prop of the declining stage." Never was the drama in higher repute: the theatre might in fact be called the temple of England at this period. The best of her public writers, like Addison and Johnson, aspired to its honors. What must have been the respect of the people for the church when, among the clergy, could be found men like Swift and Sterne to regale the gross taste of the age with ribald burlesque and licentious humor? And what were the popular fictions of the day? Peregrine Pickle, Roderick Random, Tom Jones, and Joseph Andrews The names of Smollet and Fielding obtained a renown which renders them still familiar; while that of Richardson, who, as Johnson says, "was as superior to them in talents as in virtue," is barely remembered. These were the parlor-table books of the age, while on the same table lay also the Metamorphoses, translated by the wits of the period, with Dryden at their head, dedicated to the first ladies of the court, embellished with illustrations which modern delicacy would hardly tolerate, and teeming with the sensual pruriency which pervades the polite writings of that and the preceding age. Dryden died at the beginning of the century, and his writings, as full of vice as of genius, were in general vogue. The infidel works of Hobbes, Tindal, Shaftsbury, and Chubb, were in full circulation, and were powerfully reinforced by the appearance of the three greatest giants in the cause of speculative error which modern times have produced—Bolingbroke, Hume, and Gibbon—the first influential by his political eminence and political partisans, and by the adornments which the harmonious verse of Pope gave to his sentiments; the second by all the arts of insinuation, and by a style which, says Sir J. Mackintosh, "was more lively, more easy, more ingratiating, and, if the word may be so applied, more amusing than that of any other metaphysical writer;" and the last by weaving his perverse opinions into one of the greatest works of the human intellect, a production as corrupt in its sentiments as it is magnificent in its execution. The intelligent reader need not be reminded that the same class of writers had triumphed, and were at this time in full prevalence, across the channel. The Encyclopedists had attempted the infernal project of eradicating from the whole circle of the sciences every trace of Christian truth; and the polite writers of France, headed by Voltaire and Rousseau, had decked the corrupt doctrines of the day with all the attractions of eloquence and poetry, humor and satire, until they swept, like a sirocco in tempest, over the nation, withering, not only the sentiments of religion, but the instincts of humanity, and subverting, at last, in common ruin, the altar, the throne, and the sacred protections of domestic life. Notwithstanding the inveterate antipathies which existed between the two nations, the contagion of French opinions, both in religion and politics, infected England seriously during most of the eighteenth century.

It is worthy of remark that one of the most interesting departments of the English literature of the last century owes its birth to the alarm which the better-disposed literati of the age took at the general declension of manners and morals, and their attempt to check it. I refer to the *Periodical Essay*. The *British Essayists* are technically distinguished in our literature. They form a department which has become classical. A foreign writer says that they have been reprinted more extensively than any other books in our language, except the Scriptures. Some of the brightest names in the catalogue of English writers owe much of their fame to these works. Among them may be mentioned Steele, Addison, Berkeley, and Johnson.

These publications, which afterward became so distinguished, were conducted as ephemeral sheets. They were issued twice or thrice a week, and contained brief articles, which discussed the follies and vices of the times. Their character was generally humorous or sarcastic: occasionally they contained a sober rebuke of the irreligion of the day. The first in the list is the *Tattler*, projected by Steele, but to which Addison was a frequent contributor. It s almost exclusively confined to the superficial defects of society. It is the best picture extant of the domestic, moral, and literary condition of the early part of that century. The *Spectator*, conducted conjointly by Addison and Steele, followed the Tattler. It is still one of the most popular works of our language; and presents, perhaps, one of the best standards of correct English style which we possess. Next appeared the *Guardian*, projected by Steele, but aided much by Addison, Pope, and Berkeley. A long list of miscellaneous writers of the same class followed, who have not been placed, by public opinion, in the rank of the classical essayists. Dr. Johnson, in his *Rambler*, restored the periodical essay to its first dignity.

I have already mentioned that these writers aimed, at first, more at the correction of the follies than the sins of the times. They grew serious, however, as they grew important. It is curious to observe their increasing severity, as they obtained authority by time and popularity.

Steele, from a long and various study of the world, painted, with minute accuracy, its absurdities. Addison, with a style the most pure, and a humor mild and elegant, attempted to correct the literary taste of the times, and to shed the radiance of genius on the despised virtues of Christianity. He rescued Milton from neglect. He exemplified in death the power of his principles. Pope satirized, in some admirable critiques, the literary follies of the day. Berkeley attacked, with his clear logic and finished style, the skeptical opinions which were then prevalent. Most of his articles are on "Freethinking;" and Johnson, " the great moralist," stood up a giant to battle, with both hands, against all error and irreligion, whether in high places or low places.

These writings exerted an influence upon the tastes and morals of the age; but it was comparatively superficial. Gay, who was contemporary with Addison and Steele, says, "It is incredible to conceive the effect they have had on the town; how many thousand follies they have either quite banished or given a very great check to; how much countenance they have added to virtue and religion; how many they have rendered happy by showing that it was their own fault if they were not so." Miss H. More has devoted a chapter in her Education of a Princess to this interesting portion of our literature. She speaks in the highest terms of Addison's influence, and confirms my statements of the age:—" At a period when religion was held in more than usual contempt, from its having been recently abused to the worst purposes, and when the higher walks of life exhibited that dissoluteness which the profligate reign of the second Charles has made so deplorably fashionable, Addison seems to have been raised up by Providence for the double purpose of improving the public taste and correcting the public morals. As the powers of imagination had, in the preceding age, been peculiarly abused to the purposes of vice, it was Addison's great object to show that vice and impurity have no necessary connection with genius. He not only evinced this by his reasonings, but he so exemplified it by his own compositions as to become, in a short time, more generally useful, by becoming more popular, than any writer who had yet appeared. This well-earned celebrity he endeavored to turn to the best of all purposes; and his success was such as to prove that genius is never so advantageously employed as in the service of virtue—no influence so well directed as in rendering piety fashionable."

While I commend these writers for the elevated purpose which they proposed, a purpose noble as it was novel among what are called polite writers, I repeat that their influence was comparatively superficial—it was infinitely short of what was necessary—it was moral, but not spiritual. It was on the side of Christianity, but had nothing to do with those great evangelical truths which are the vital elements of Christianity, in which inheres its renovating energy. It is the diffusion of these truths among the popular mass that alone can effect any general and permanent elevation of man. It was reserved for the agency of Methodism to revive and spread them, with a transforming efficacy, through the British empire and most of the civilized world. I have referred to these writers, therefore, only as evidences of the conviction, felt by the better-disposed literary leaders of the day, that some new check was necessary to stop the overwhelming progress of vice. The pictures of vice which they exhibit, and the manner in which they attempt the necessary reform, show that society was not only deplorably wicked, but that the adequate means of its recovery were not under stood by those who lamented its evils. But let us turn our attention to other views of the subject.

There is abundant testimony that I have not exaggerated the degeneracy of the period referred to. The writings which have been described reflect, as in a mirror, its morals, and we can scarcely detect a single evidence that spiritual Christianity was at all *comprehended* by the mass, and, perhaps, no better by the elevated few. I speak of that which constitutes the speciality of religion as a regenerating energy, a system of internal spiritual virtues, of which forms and morals are not the substance, but the spontaneous manifestation, as the light of day is but the effusion of the burning centre of radiation.

Natural religion was the favorite study of the clergy, and included most of their theology. Arianism and Socinianism, propagated by such men as Dr. S. Clarke, Priestley, and Whiston, were becoming fashionable among the learned, and Calvinism was tending, with full speed, to Antinomianism. Some of the brightest names of the times can be quoted as exceptions to these remarks; but this was the general condition of religion in England. The higher classes laughed at piety, and prided themselves on being above what they called the infection of its fanaticism; the lower classes were grossly ignorant, and abandoned to vice; while the church, enervated by a universal decline, was unable any longer to give countenance to the downfallen cause of truth.

This general decline had reached its extremity when Wesley and his coadjutors appeared. "It was," to use his own words, "just at the time when we wanted little of filling up the measure of our iniquities, that two or three clergymen of the Church of England began vehemently to call sinners to repentance." His own testimony to the irreligion of the times is truly appalling. "What," he asks, "is the present characteristic of the English nation? It is ungodliness. This is at present the characteristic of the English nation. Ungodliness is our universal, our constant, our peculiar character. A total ignorance of God is almost universal among us. The exceptions are exceedingly few, both among the learned and the unlearned. High and low are as ignorant of the Creator of the world as Mohammedans or pagans." Let not these fearful statements be condemned as *ex parte*. Those who are entitled to be classed among the enemies of this extraordinary man confirm them. Southey says, "The clergy had lost that authority which may always command, at least, the appearance of respect; and they had lost that respect also by which the place of authority may sometimes so much more worthily be supplied. For the loss of power they were not censurable; but if they possessed but little of that influence which the minister who diligently and conscientiously discharges his duty will certainly acquire, it is manifest that as a body they must have been culpably remiss. In the great majority of the clergy zeal was wanting. The excellent Leighton spoke of the church as a fair carcass without a spirit. Burnet observes that, in his time, our clergy had less authority, and were under more contempt, than those of any other church in all Europe; for they were much the most remiss in their labors, and the least severe in their lives. It was not that their lives were scandalous; he entirely acquitted them of any such imputation; but they were not exemplary, as it became them to be; and, in the sincerity of a pious and reflecting mind, he pronounced that they would never regain the influence they had lost till they lived better and labored more."

The best contemporary authorities confirm these statements, and do so with an emphasis which cannot but strike us as remarkable. Dr.

Watts declares that there was "a general decay of vital religion in the hearts and lives of men;" that "this declension of piety and virtue" was common among dissenters and churchmen; that it was "a general matter of mournful observation among all who lay the cause of God to heart;" and he calls upon "every one" to use all possible efforts for "*the recovery of dying religion in the world.*" Another writer asserts that "the Spirit of God has so far departed from the nation, that hereby almost all vital religion is lost out of the world." Another author says, "The present modish turn of religion looks as if we had no need of a Mediator, but that all our concerns with God were managed with him as an absolute God. The religion of nature makes up the darling topics of our age; and the religion of Jesus is valued only for the sake of that, and only so far as it carries on the light of nature, and is a bare improvement of that kind of light. All that is restrictively Christian, or that is peculiar to Christ—everything concerning him that has not its apparent foundation in natural light, or that goes beyond its principles—is waived, and banished, and despised."

The venerable Burnet speaks on this subject with a pathos truly affecting.: "I am now in my seventieth year. I cannot speak long in the vorld, therefore I lay hold on the present time to give free vent to those sad thoughts that lie on my mind both day and night, and are the subject of many secret mournings." He declares, he " cannot look on, without the deepest concern, when he sees *the imminent ruin which hangs over the church;* and this *ruin*," he asserts, " threatens *the whole reformation*." "The outward state of things is bleak enough, God knows; but that which heightens my fears rises chiefly from the inward state into which we are unhappily fallen!"

Archbishop Secker says, " In this we cannot be mistaken, that an open and professed disregard is become, through a variety of unhappy causes, the distinguishing character of the present age." " Such," he declares, " are the dissoluteness and contempt of principle in the higher part of the world, and the profligacy, intemperance, and fearlessness of committing crimes, in the lower, as must, if this torrent of impiety stop not, become absolutely fatal." He further asserts that "Christianity is ridiculed and railed at with very little reserve, and the teachers of it without any at all ;" and this testimony was made but one year before that which is commemorated as the original year of Methodism. About this same time Butler published his unparalleled work on the Analogy between Religion and the Constitution and Course of Nature. In his preface he gives a deplorable description of the religious world. He concurs with the preceding authorities in representing it in the very extreme of decline. " It has come to be taken for granted that Christianity is no longer a subject of inquiry; but that it is now at length discovered to be fictitious. And accordingly it is treated as if, in the present age, this were an agreed point among all persons of discernment, and nothing remained but to set it up a principal subject for mirth and ridicule."

I have been the more minute on this subject because, as a church, we have been accused of arrogance in ascribing too much importance to the influence of Methodism. When it is considered that it found the Christian world in this perilous extremity, and that the contrast which the present state of Protestant Christendom exhibits has been subsequently effected, perhaps the liability of exaggeration will not be so strongly suspected.

The rise of Methodism, under these circumstances, presents a most sublime instance of moral triumph, and of the deathless energy of those great principles which Christianity has set in operation for the regeneration of the world; and which prophecy, through many weary ages, and in many dark intervals, when their radiance has seemed almost extinguished, and their efficacy exhausted, has still, with unfaltering emphasis, pronounced to be invincible. Let good men learn not to despair, and the foes of Christianity not to hope, in the hour of her trial. The sun, when his rays are intercepted by clouds, is not annihilated, but still wheels on in his chariot of fire above the darkness and the storm, and, when they have subsided, bursts with but greater splendor on the world. The whole history of religion teaches the lesson of confidence to its friends, and of failure to its enemies. Its triumphant delivery in its patriarchal form, in Egypt; its extraordinary and victorious struggle with classic Polytheism, throughout the Roman empire; its successful conflict with the stupendous superstitions of Popery, when it dissipated the darkness of ten centuries; and its renovation under Wesley, when it combated and overcame polished skepticism, learned heterodoxy, and general irreligion, —all show that, however dark its occasional obscuration may be, it possesses an inherent power of self-renovation which allows no final hope to its opposers. At the very moment when Bishop Butler penned the above fearful description of the English Church, and skeptics were congratulating themselves with the thought that Christianity was expiring in its dotage, the "holy club," at Oxford, were kindling a fire which, in the words of an English reformer to his fellow-martyr, at the stake, was to "put all England in a blaze;" and which is still extending, like flame in stubble, through the length and breadth of the world. God was preparing, at this time, Wesley, Whitefield, and their coadjutors, to meet the crisis; and, on the clouds of that dark period he wrote, as with their own lightning, the date of a new epoch in the history of the church. Protestant Christendom has been partially regenerated since that period; and nearly the whole series of benevolent institutions which are now redeeming the world sprang up from its darkness.

2

BISHOP ASBURY AND BLACK PUNCH.

"A word in season."—Isaiah.

One of the greatest misfortunes of our denominational literature is that we have no biography of Bishop Asbury. What a life was his! What a diversified delineation would his history be! And yet it is not the great deeds of that great man—his vast journeyings, incessant preaching, and executive plans—that illustrate fully his character; he that would write a genuine biography of Asbury must gather from all the wide-spread country the numerous incidents, of his more personal life, the anecdotes and sayings that exhibit characteristically the man.

One of these, an affecting fact in itself, as well as an illustration of the bishop's character, occurred, in 1798, on his journey to Charleston, S. C. He passed a creek, in the parish of St——, on the bank of which sat a slave fishing and humming a ditty; his name was Punch. He was notorious for his vicious character. The good bishop on riding toward him, bethought himself that under that squalid exterior lived an immortal spirit for whom Christ had died, and the salvation of which would be a higher achievement than the conquest of a world. Such were familiar thoughts to that great mind. He stopped his horse, and entered into conversation with the negro.

"Do you ever pray, my friend?" inquired the bishop.

"No sir," replied Punch.

The bishop deliberately proceeded to alight, fasten his horse to a tree, and seat himself by the side of the slave.

Punch was evidently astonished at the good man's conduct, but was relieved immediately by the kindness of his tones. He commenced a minute conversation with him on religion, explaining the nature and consequences of sin, the atonement, repentance, justification by faith, the certainty of death, the terrors of the judgment and hell. The bishop, earnest for the rescue of this benighted, but immortal spirit, warmed into exhortation and entreaty. Punch soon began to feel, tears ran down his sable cheeks, he seemed deeply alarmed at his danger, and listened with intenseness to the counsels of the singular stranger.

After a long conversation the bishop sung the hymn,—

"Plunged in a gulf of dark despair."—

prayed with him, and pursued his journey, doubtless thinking of and praying for the poor slave as he measured the miles of his tedious route.

More than twenty years elapsed before he saw again or heard anything of Punch. While on another visit to Charleston he was called upon by an aged and Christian negro, who had obtained permission from his master to visit him, and had traveled seventy miles on foot for the purpose. It was the slave he had warned and prayed over on the bank of the creek, and who had ever since been journeying on the way to heaven. What a lesson must this interview have taught the apostolic bishop! What an encouragement to labor and pray for the salvation of souls under the most forbidding circumstances!

The bishop had no sooner left Punch on the bank of the stream than he took up his fishing tackle and hastened home in the deepest agitation of mind, pondering over the words of the venerable man.

The divine Spirit was operating upon his dark mind, new light, new thoughts, stirring the depths of the soul, had dawned upon him. He endeavored to conform to the instructions he had received, and when some days of anguish and prayer had elapsed, he found peace in believing, and became a new man. The change was too manifest not to be discovered by his fellow-servants—it was the topic of his conversation with them incessantly. In his simple way he pointed them to the Lamb of God which taketh away the sins of the world, and though they lived at a time when religious instruction was rare among slaves, yet they comprehended the novel tale, and many of them became thoroughly penitent for their sins, and, guided by the Spirit of grace, found "the knowledge of salvation by the remission of sins through faith in Christ Jesus." The interest extended from one to another, and throngs of the neglected Africans resorted to his humble cabin to receive his exhortations and prayers.

Several remarkable results followed, one of which was the conversion of a perverse overseer who had charge of the plantation. This man, perceiving the increasing interest of the slaves for their souls, and their constant attendance in the evenings at Punch's cabin, determined to put a stop to the spreading leaven He forbade Punch to hold religious meetings among them; he was, therefore, confined in his Christian labors to those who belonged to his own cabin, and a few immediately adjacent, who clandestinely met with him when they could with safety. One evening, when the little band were praying together, the overseer's voice was heard without, loudly calling for Punch. They were all terrified, suspecting that he had discovered them, and was summoning their devoted guide to a severe chastisement. Punch went out; but he found the overseer on his knees under a tree, alternately supplicating the mercy of God, and calling on the poor slave to pray for him. God's Spirit, probably by the example of these converted negroes, had got hold upon his conscience. His attempt to suppress their meetings could not suppress his convictions; they deepened, and at last, overpowering him, led him to seek relief in prayer under the tree, and there they constrained him to implore the sympathies and prayers of poor Punch. The negroes gathered around him and prayed with him till God, in his mercy, pardoned and comforted him. The overseer now became a coworker with Punch among them; he joined the nearest Methodist Church, and, in time, became an exhorter, and finally a preacher!

Punch had now full liberty to do good among his associates. He exhorted, prayed, and led them on, as a shepherd his flock, and extended his usefulness around the whole neighborhood. After many years he was removed, by the decease of his master and the distribution of the estate, to the parish of A., where he continued to labor for the souls of his fellow-bondsmen with still greater success. Scores, and even hundreds, were converted through his instrumentality. He sustained a kind of pastoral charge over them for several years. The preacher from whom we have these particulars was the first missionary who found them out. He writes: "In 1836, at the special solicitation of planters of that particular section of country, a missionary was sent to their plantations from the South Carolina Conference. I was honored with the appointment. On my reaching the plantation where Punch lived, I found between two and three hundred persons under his spiritual supervision, who had been gathered into a kind of society; many of whom, upon further acquaintance, I discovered to be truly pious and consistent. I was much interested on my first visit to the old veteran. Just before I reached his house, I met a herdsman, and asked him if there was any preacher on the plantation. 'O yes, massa, de ole bushup lib here!' 'Is he a good preacher?' said I. 'O yes,' was the reply, 'he ward burn we heart!' He showed me the house. I knocked at the door, and heard approaching footsteps and the sound of a cane upon the floor. The door opened, and I saw before me, leaning upon a staff, a hoary-headed black man, with palsied limbs, but a smiling face. He looked at me for a moment in silence; then, raising his hands and eyes to heaven, he said, 'Now, Lord, lettest thou thy servant depart in peace, for mine eyes have seen thy salvation.' I was confused. He asked me to take a seat; and I found in the following remarks the reason of his exclamation. Said he, 'I have many children in this place. I have felt, for some time past, that my end was nigh. I have looked around to see who might take my place when I am gone. I could find no one. I felt unwilling to die and leave them so, and have been praying to God to send some one to take care of them. The Lord has sent you, my child; I am now ready to go.' Tears coursed freely down his time-shriveled face. I was overwhelmed.

"'This interview gave me much encouragement. He had heard of the application for a missionary, and only wanted to live long enough to see his face. After this I had several interviews with him, from which I learned his early history. I always found him contented and happy. Some time afterward he was taken ill, and lingered a few days. On a sabbath morning he told me he thought he should die that day. He addressed affecting words to the people who crowded around his dying bed; the burden of his remarks—the theme of his soul, was, 'Now, Lord, lettest thou thy servant depart in peace!' He applied these words to himself, and continued his address to the last moment; and death gently stole his spirit away while saying, 'Let thy servant depart in peace —let—let—le!'

"His mistress sent for me to preach his funeral sermon. The corpse was decently shrouded, and the coffin was carried to the house of worship. I looked upon the face of the cold clay. The departed spirit had left the impress of heaven upon it. Could I be at a loss for a text? I read out of the Gospel, 'Now, Lord, lettest thou thy servant depart in peace.'"

Blessed be God for the saving power of his word and Spirit! This poor negro, vicious and ignorant, appealed to by a passing ambassador of Christ, is pierced to the heart, and, without subsequent guidance from man, becomes, by the renewal of the Holy Ghost, a child of God, an heir of glory—the instrument of the conversion of his persecutor, and the spiritual guide of hundreds of African converts! and goes up at last, in glorious ascension, to the "heavenly

Jerusalem, the innumerable company of angels!"

And what an example does this incident furnish to the doers of good! Many would probably have passed by the benighted bondman at the brook, as did the priest and Levite the wounded man on the way to Jericho. But the human spirit, habited in rags, and deformed by ignorance and vice, is as valuable in the estimation of angels, as when clothed with the regalia of thrones; and such should be its estimation by all Christ's followers. How, then, should they "be instant, in season and out of season," becoming all things to all men, that they may save some!

This act of usefulness is a striking illustration of Asbury's character—a higher certificate of his apostleship than could be the loftiest abilities of the pulpit, or the most pompous imposition of prelatical hands. Who can doubt that, in heaven, it will be signalized for its results more than any of those polemical displays or powers of ecclesiastical leadership which procure the fame of greatness on earth? If I ever reach the better world, I expect to see this greatest of modern bishops walking the golden streets with the redeemed slave by his side, one of his noblest trophies!

A THEOLOGICAL SKETCH.

"Men ought always to pray."—Christ.

I HAVE heard to-day a discourse on the excellency of prayer. The subject possesses a logical importance and a practical grandeur which interested me much, and induce me to record some of its outlines.

If our world, said the preacher, had rolled on until this date in its present depravity, and that agony of moral wo which yet overspreads it; and if it had possessed a less perfect revelation, one which afforded a true knowledge of its lost condition, and the awful character of God, but no notion of access to him by prayer, through the merits of an atonement; if it, at this moment, were in such a state—trembling under the knowledge of God without daring to look up unto him—groping through a half-illuminated darkness, in which the realities of present wretchedness could be seen, but not the hopes of future relief; what would be the effect of a proclamation made convincingly to the whole earth, say by an apparition of angels in the firmament, as once in the plains of Bethlehem, that *on a given day God would hear prayer*, and that supplication, offered on terms practicable to all, should secure any blessing truly appropriate to man, and should avail for the blessedness of the suppliant, even through everlasting ages? What amazement and exultation would such an event spread through the world! How would the hours and moments which were yet to precede that day be counted! How would the fiiends of the sick, by the virtue of medicines, and by tender cares, try to preserve the flickering existence, that the dying beloved one might pray before he departed, and the aged and despairing, who have longed for the grave, seek to prolong their lives to the auspicious morning! Surely such a proclamation, under such circumstances, would be like the trump of resurrection to the saints, and the emotions of mankind would be like those of the despairing lunatic, when some beautiful dream deludes his sleep, and mingles smiles and tears on his haggard countenance. Would any sleep the last night which was to precede it? And what a sight would the sun of that day witness in his course around the earth, of prostrate, grateful, imploring millions!

Such, it is probable, would be the effect of novelty in a privilege which, now, because it is always at our command, is reluctantly improved by many, and utterly rejected by most. How absurd, us well as guilty, is sin! How valuable, though unvalued, the privileges of the gospel! A lost spirit would give all worlds to be placed in the probationary position of a living sinner; and if the hope of salvation were to be limited to one day, instead of being continued through years; if, in other words, to-morrow were to be the judgment, the sun of this day would go down amid the tears and prayers of the world.

Yet independently of such illustrations, and depreciated as the privilege of prayer is by our desultory familiarity with it, to what thoughtful mind does it not present itself as one of the most wonderful and precious institutions of religion!

Prayer is a reasonable exercise. This, said the preacher, can be best shown by examining those speculative objections which have been preferred by skeptics against it. He examined these, and refuted them thoroughly.

One, said he, is, That prayer is inconsistent with the divine *omniscience.* "If God knows your wants, and your disposition to have them supplied, why inform and importune him in prayer?" The objection proceeds from a misapprehension of the *design* of prayer. Its *ostensible* design is indeed the attainment of the blessing for which we pray; but there is an *ulterior* and higher object for which it was appointed, namely, the spiritual influence, the *disciplinary effect* of the habit. The objection would apply equally to the other departments of God's economy. He could make bread grow spontaneously, or drop manna from heaven, but he requires man to toil for his sustenance. He could have constituted the human mind so, that its improvement might be natural, not the result of protracted study; but he has not, and why? because he saw it would be good for man to co-operate with himself in procuring improvement and happiness. The analogy applies equally to religion, to prayer. Hence, after predicting to Israel certain mercies, God still declares, "I will yet for this be inquired of by the house of Israel to do it for them." Man's measures contemplate, usually, but a specific object, God's contemplate many at once. The apparent design of the sun is to illuminate the world, "to rule the day;" but, on closer examination, this is found to be only one among many of its agencies—while it enlightens, it also beautifies nature with coloring; it is essential to vegetation; it varies the seasons; it sustains in harmonious motion the stupendous machinery of our whole system. So in God's moral economy, manifold results, ostensible and ulterior, are accomplished. Thus is it with prayer.

Another objection alledges that prayer is inconsistent with God's *immutability*. "Why entreat and importune him? you cannot charge his immutable nature." Here is a misapprehension of the divine immutability. God is immutable in the *principles* of his administration, but not in its *acts*. There was a period when he did not create, one when he did create, and one when "he rested from all his work which he had made:" he changed in act, but not in nature. The laws protect you to-day because you conform to them, to-morrow they may put you to death for transgressing them; not because they change—the change is in yourself. So the sinner is heard if he truly prays, but lost if he prays not; yet God does not change, it is his ordained and immutable economy that it should be so.

It is asserted again that the universe is governed by *secondary causes*, and in order that prayer should bring about results different from what would take place without it, there must be an interference with—a suspension of those fixed causes; but we see no such interference. The objection assumes that we see the whole series of causes and effects; but that series, extending from the effect which we observe up to the first cause, is immense. We notice but the lowest links in the chain; how then can we assume that the higher ones are not adapted or controlled so as to meet this peculiarity of the moral system? The last link of the series is in the hand of Omnipotence. Why may not the divine energy be transmitted down through the whole, with almighty power, and yet with no interruption of the successive links; as the electric energy passes with quickening or overpowering influence to the object at the end of the chain, without visible effect on the intermediate links? Behold the mighty machinery of the steamer: the effect of a man's hand can reverse its course, and carry the immense structure backward, without a collision of the works; and cannot the Maker of the worlds so control his works as to bring about, without confusion, results different from what our little minds judge necessary to the instruments which he has appointed?

Another objection is our comparative insignificance. "Can it be supposed that the infinite God can stoop from amid all worlds to regard our wants and prayers?" Yes, said the preacher, the greatness of God, the very ground of the objection, is the ground of our confidence. God is *infinite;* were he finite, however great there might be plausibility in the objection: but infinite greatness implies that the small as well as the great, the minutiæ as well as the aggregate—that all things are comprehended by it. Were there a particle of sand not pervaded by God's presence, then he would not be omnipresent. Did the smallest animalcule escape his cognizance, then he could not be omniscient; his Godhead would be destroyed. The arrow that misses the mark by the distance of an inch, misses it as really as if by a hundred feet. Infinite knowledge implies the cognizance of not merely the universe at large, but, definitely, of every minute thing in it. The sigh of penitence that goes up from a dying bed, in the lowliest hovel, or from the dungeon of the prisoner, enters into the ears of the Lord God of Sabbaoth, amid the hallelujahs of all the heavens. It is noticed by him as distinctly as if it were the only sound in his universe. It is as much the necessity as it is the mercy of God's nature that a sparrow cannot fall to the ground without his notice. Thus, then, these four speculative difficulties vanish, and prayer may be affirmed to be a *reasonable exercise.*

Prayer is a salutary exercise. It is so, in the first place, because it is the *means* of the blessings prayed for. Faith is the condition of salvation; it is faith that is imputed for righteousness; yet prayer is the expression, the vehicle of faith; prayer is the wing on which faith rises to the mercy-seat. The affirmation is as true in regard to prayer as it is in regard to faith—that no responsible sinner has ever been saved without it. God has not made it one of the conditions of salvation, yet it is an inseparable appliance to those conditions. In the second place, the disciplinary effect is salutary. We have already, said the preacher, viewed this aspect of the subject, but it is worthy of another glance: "We find," says a distinguished writer, "from the whole course of nature, that God governs the world not by independent acts, but by a connected system. The instruments which he employs in the ordinary works of his providence are not physically necessary to his operations. He might have acted without them if he pleased. He might, for instance, have created all men without the intervention of parents; but where, then, had been the beneficial connection between parents and children, and the numerous advantages resulting to human society from such connections? The difficulty lies here: the *uses* arising from the *connections* of God's acts may be various; and such are the pregnancies of his works, that *a single act* may answer a prodigious variety of purposes. Of these several purposes we are, for the most part, ignorant; and from this ignorance are derived most of our weak objections against the ways of his providence; while we foolishly presume that, like human agents, he has but one end in view." Now the effect of prayer, aside from its particular object, may be among these several purposes. How can it fail to be thus salutary, when the first impression it gives the mind is that of dependence? If our spiritual blessings were matters of course, and not of condition, like the blessings of light, air, or water, we would forget, as the world has in regard to the latter, the merciful agency of God in conferring them. Prayer, therefore, tends to *humility. Gratitude*, likewise, is produced by it in the same manner. There is no virtuous affection with which it is not congenial. It is serene, tranquilizing, spiritualizing. It cannot consist with sin. "Prayer," says one, "will make us either cease sinning, or sin make us cease praying."

Prayer is a consolatory exercise. Man has a moral nature. His moral faculties are as distinguishable and as constitutional as his physical or intellectual. His most perfect happiness consists in the due gratification of all his faculties. But most of mankind limit this gratification to the physical nature. A few, "of soul more elevate," add the pleasures of intellect. Yet the highest demand of our nature remains unanswered. The greatest monsters, not only of crime but of misery, have been sensualists; and the highest intellectual powers have aided only in removing the illusions of worldly pleasure, and overclouding the soul with disgust and despair, so that a philosopher has said, that "a fool may, but a philosopher cannot, be a happy man." Our moral wants are our largest, and most urgent ones, and their neglect explains the existence of wretchedness amid every other gratification—in the palace as well as the hovel, with the sovereign and the sage as well as the pauper and the slave. There is a higher gratification than that of sense; there is a higher exercise than that of thought. It is the satisfaction of the conscience, and the exercise of the heart. God made man for intercourse with himself; all other exercises and enjoyments were to be but secondary to this. Prayer is the means of this intercourse, its language is the converse of this communion.

But it is consolatory in a second sense; it is a source of aid and security. The supplicating accents of prayer are authoritative to command for our aid the very attributes of the Deity. Prayer is the eloquence that persuades God. What would be the consciousness of a man invested with the attributes of the Almighty—omniscience to discern every danger, omnipotence to avert it, and a capability of universal presence to exert everywhere his wisdom and power for his interests! How fearlessly would he throw himself on every emergency! How tranquilly walk through every peril! Now the Christian has not these attributes, but his God has, and that God pledges their interference for him, in answer to prayer, in every case where their interference will be for his interests! that is, in every case where the Christian would exercise them himself, were he possessed of them. He may therefore feel as secure as if the powers of Godhead were at his command! These powers may allow him to suffer, but no more than he himself would allow, if he had infinite wisdom to discern the propriety of such suffering. How sublime a spectacle is the praying man in this light! The stars may fall and the worlds pass away, but he is safe, for the power which dissolves them, supports him. A devout mind, constant in the habit of prayer, may acquire such a lively sense of the immediate presence and sympathy of God as to exult in the most trying danger and be almost superior to even the instinctive fears of human nature.

Prayer is a sublime exercise. The reach of a mighty mind, transcending the discoveries of ages, and evoking to view new principles or new worlds, is sublime. Newton's discoveries, pushing human comprehension higher in the series of natural causes and effects, were sublime. But there may be a progress remaining, compared with which, his discoveries, as he said himself, are like the bubble compared with the ocean. But prayer sweeps over all secondary causes, and lays hold on the first cause; it bends not its flight to repose its wing and refresh itself amid the light of undiscovered worlds, but rises above the stars and suns, until it bathes its pinions in the light of " the excellent glory." To control the tremendous force of the elements, and reduce them to the servility of mechanical operations, is a sublime achievement Men can thereby float in palaces on seas, carried by whirlwinds over fleeing mountains, or drive carriages, burdened with armies, through valleys and through hills, without animal effort, and as swift almost as light. But what is the control of the elements compared with the ability of prayer to call down the powers of heaven, and summon the agency of angels! I would be a circumstance of great sublimity for a man to be able to transmit his thoughts to a distant planet, and hold communion with its inhabitants; but prayer aspires above all worlds, and communes with Infinite Mind. It rises above every subordinate reliance, and stops not till it throws itself into the embrace of the Father of all. One of the indirect, but salutary, effects of prayer arises from this sublime ascension of the soul above all things limited, or caused, to the infinite. It approaches God; it stops only when all things else are lost from view, and the effulgence of divinity alone shines "above, beneath, around." The mind cannot but imbibe sublimity from such a scene. A praying man ought, indeed, to be sublime—sublime in his sentiments and in his purposes; he holds perpetual intercourse with all grandeur. If the study of greatness, in its historical examples; if association with living men of greatness; if the intercourse of archangels, could tend to enlarge and elevate our sentiments, how much more ought the habitual contemplation and communion of God to improve us!

MOTHER SUMA AND THE WEALTHY CONVERT.

"*The elect lady.*"—John.

A NUMBER of years ago, when the now venerable Bishop H—— was stationed in Boston, he was surprised one morning by the call, at the parsonage, of a lady whose costly dress, and elegant manners, indicated that she belonged to the highest circles of the polished society of that polished city. He was still more surprised when, after the usual introductory phrases, she made known, with language direct and decided, her wish to unite with the humble society under his charge. She gave him her name, and the highest references in the city, for information respecting her, and retired with an earnest request, that he would consider the application till she should be able to have another interview.

This lady was a near relative of the celebrated John Hancock, whose name stands so prominently on the Declaration of Independence, and in the history of his country. At the time of her visit at the Methodist parsonage she was surrounded with all the resources and gayeties of her high sphere in life; but that blessed Spirit, which "is given to all men," had been striving with her mind, and had made use of an instrumentality to lead her to the church, and to heaven, so remarkable as to deserve notice and commemoration. While living in luxury, with no higher notions of religion than those afforded by the fashionable Unitarianism of the day, the providence of God placed in her family a devoted Methodist servant-maid, to whom was afterward added also, in occasional service in the household, a pious colored woman, of the same denomination.

The religious example and converse of these humble Christians could not escape the observation of the lady of the house; they were unostentatious ministries which God had placed there, and with the exercise of which he honors his lowliest saints, while he withholds it from the angels of heaven. Their mistress became interested and thoughtful; she picked up one of their books; it was a volume of Wesley's Sermons. She opened at the discourse on "The Witness of the Spirit:" what a mystical phrase! She had never heard of it in her own church; but on reading the *text* it appeared obviously a proper—a Scriptural title. She read the sermon through; it poured a flood of light upon her neglected spirit; if this was religion, she had never known it by experience. She read the whole volume: it explained to her, for the first time in her life, the true character of personal piety, and led her to the mercy-seat to seek it. Her deep and anxious convictions of sin were revealed to her devoted servants, and these lowly children of God, while laboring in her kitchen, became her instructors and guides in the way to heaven. She longed to hear a genuine minister of Christ who preached these new truths, and several evenings might be seen this votary of the fashionable world, still arrayed in her gay apparel, following at a short distance, and with a throbbing heart, her humble colored servant to the Methodist chapel. There she heard the same truths vivified by the living voice; their impression on her conscience was deepened; she sought with all her soul the pardoning mercy of God. In a few weeks she was "justified by faith, and had peace with God through our Lord Jesus Christ."

She had thus far kept her exercises of mind a profound secret, known only to herself and her pious servants; she felt now that it was her duty, and her only safety, to openly confess Christ, and associate herself with his people. Too precious were the new truths and new sympathies which had dawned upon her soul to allow her to seek a fashionable religious communion, where the reproach of the cross might be evaded; the humble but devoted people, whose agency had reached her, and led her to "the Lamb of God which taketh away the sins of the world," were her decided choice, and she called upon their pastor, as stated, to solicit admission to their lowly fellowship.

In a few days she visited him again: he had consulted her references, and ascertained her high family relations and excellent character. No misfortune, or eccentricity of mind, could account for her decided predilection for the Methodist Church. She had been renewed in spirit, had consecrated herself to God, and intent only on the salvation of her soul, resolved to place herself amid such religious associations as would most effectually enable her to work out her salvation with fear and trembling, and she justly inferred that the obscurity and poverty of the then little Methodist band would but render her connection with them a more exemplary proof of her love of their Redeemer, and increase her facilities for usefulness. Mr H. informed her that there could be no objection to her reception among them; but assured her of the disparity between her circumstances and habits and those of most of his people. He explained to her also the disciplinary rules of dress.

Her reply was, that she had read the Discipline; had counted the cost, and was ready to conform to it. She was afterward publicly received at the altar of the church, attired in that chaste and beautiful simplicity which our Discipline and the spirit of our religion require, and, above all, with that spirit of meekness, that beauty of holiness, which form the loveliness of piety on earth, and of angels in heaven.

She was ever after distinguished by eminent piety, and all its graceful fruits. In the church she found, as she had calculated, a useful field for her talents and resources. Her time was devoted to unostentatious charities. Not long after her remarkable change, the decease of her husband placed a large fortune entirely at her own command. She then consecrated herself to more abundant usefulness; the poor, the sick, the widow, and the fatherless, and all the benevolent claims of the church, were the objects of her sympathy and liberality. Thus rejoicing in the hope of the glory of God herself, and dispensing happiness all around her, life became to her a scene of the purest blessedness. Ah, if the rich and the fashionable who, with satiated tastes and aching hearts, are ever turning from, and anon returning to, the hollow gayeties of the world, could discern the serene enjoyment of the heart which throbs only to serve God and bless man, how would the attractions of frivolous pleasure change to disgust!

For three years after the death of her husband did this Christian lady thus minister, like an angel of mercy, to the necessities of the sick and the poor. At the end of this period her Lord called her to her reward. Peacefully and with holy joy she passed to the society of the good above, with the tears and blessings of those who, in humbleness of life, but with true hearts, had loved in her the similitude of their Lord. But if to do is to live, her life did not end with her death. In dying she provided for its continuance. One who has narrated the interesting facts of her short but devoted pilgrimage, says, "that she appropriated in her will a liberal share of her estate to various benevolent and religious objects." To the minister who had received her into the church, and to his colleague, she left valuable legacies, and to the church itself a perpetual fund for the use of the poor.

For the above facts I am indebted chiefly to the narrative mentioned; but it was my lot personally to witness another incident which pertains to the sketch. Many years after the departure of this "elect lady," the providence of God placed me in the pastoral charge of ——

church. Though composed of several hundred members, devoted and respectable, I found none more esteemed than an humble old colored woman, called mother Suma. Such was the purity of her Christian reputation, sustained through a long pilgrimage, that it was justly appreciated as the common and personal property of the whole church. Tranquil and uniform in her piety, faithful through many years in every duty enjoined by the church, singularly useful in her sphere, and exhibiting always those gentle affections so characteristic of the African character, her color and caste seemed forgotten in a community where they were usually strongly distinguished; she was more than respected, she was beloved. Not long after my arrival she died in great peace. I officiated at her funeral. On entering her small rooms, no one could fail to notice the impress of the good woman's mind, everything was clean and extremely neat, instinct with that expression of homely comfort so congenial to the tastes of pious old age. Here had been her retired sanctuary, the scene of her daily meditations and prayers, where she daily expected her Lord and his ministering angels, and it seemed in its whole interior aspect to have been fitted for their reception. The aged saint lay, in her coffin, in the midst of it. I was affected to see the interest of all classes to pay her memory the last acts of respect. The rooms were crowded, and throngs stood around the door unable to enter. The young were there, who had felt themselves instructed by the lessons of her holy life; the veterans of the church, who had journeyed heavenward with her from the beginning of their pilgrimage, wept around her remains; the choir, with their chorister, were there to sing the adieus of the church to the emancipated spirit which had escaped from its earthly sufferings; and as we spoke of her excellences, and prayed that her memory might be as a sweet savor among us, many hearts felt how beautiful is a holy life in even the lowliest vale of earth, and how serenely pleasant its end, and how hallowed its memory. More genuine regards accompanied that daughter of Ethiopia to the grave than attend the departure of nobles or monarchs.

The reader will share my interest in this humble saint, when I tell him that mother Suma was the colored servant who had guided the wealthy convert of the Hancock family to the Methodist chapel. As an aged member of the church was relating the fact to me, another who stood by, one of its stewards, remarked, that "the providence of God had singularly blessed the zeal of the pious African to her own advantage; that during the later and helpless years of her life she had been comfortably sustained by aid from the proceeds of the fund left by the very lady whom she had thus led into the path of life! Every month," he continued, ". for a long time, have I carried to her humble home the bounty of her deceased friend."

How marvelously does the providence of God sometimes use the feeblest means for the noblest ends! Despise not the day of small things; for "the excellency of the power is of God and not of men." And remember that in blessing others we bless ourselves; in this life we reap a reward often, in the next invariably.

DOCTRINAL CHARACTER OF METHODISM

"The apostles' doctrine."—Acts ii, 42.

Methodism was providentially distinguished as the instrument of reviving, in the church, the most important doctrines of spiritual religion. It called the attention of the Christian world anew to three great principles which comprehend the experimental divinity of the Scriptures, relating respectively to the *nature, extent,* and *evidence* of personal piety, viz., the doctrines of *justification by faith, sanctification,* and the *witness of the Spirit.* These were the great import of the ministry of Wesley and his coadjutors. They started not with the project of a new sect: this, with the disciplinary system upon which it was based, was an unexpected result: they were intent only upon shaking out of their slumbers existing sects, and replenishing the popular mind of Great Britain with the efficacious truths of the original faith.

The great truth of justification by faith, which, under Luther, startled Europe from its sleep of superstition, and produced the Reformation, was the head and front of Wesley's offending. The sermons of the day, in the national church, taught baptism as the means of regeneration.

After the sacramental initiation to the church. all that was considered requisite for salvation was a theoretical belief, and an observance of the forms and moralities of religion. Hence, when Wesley preached regeneration as a real and conscious change, effected by a supernatural influence, and procured by faith alone, he was rejected from the pulpits of London, and driven to the streets and fields. The tenet of sanctification, so explicitly taught and distinguished in the Scriptures, was involved in confusion. Its real character was unknown, and it was represented as anterior to justification. The doctrine of the witness of the Spirit, in its legitimate form, was denounced as unscriptural, and the offspring of spiritual presumption.

These were the particular doctrines insisted on by Wesley; but in reviving these he aimed at a general restoration of every department of experimental and practical religion to its primitive efficacy and vigor. He distinguished true piety from forms and morals, by declaring it to be spiritual and miraculous; a principle of inward, fervid life, attesting its divine efficacy by effects so immediate, so profound, and so uniform, under every diversity of circumstances, as to be unquestionably preternatural. By scattering thus the elements of personal piety, he expected to restore the life of public worship, and kindle afresh the smothered fires of the church altar.

In the supernatural character of Christianity consists its grand peculiarity; here is its contrast with all ethical systems, and with natural religion. *They* but teach the rules and present the motives of virtue; *this* affords the strength which is necessary for their practical use—a strength which is extraneous—which, in the sublime language of Scripture, "is sent down from heaven." It is this character of Christianity that mankind are most reluctant to concede, and most inclined to forget. This is its fanaticism, its "foolishness," and yet the rational consistency of the whole system depends upon this feature. Its fundamental truth, the inveterate depravity of our nature, which is likewise taught us by natural religion, requires this counterpart; the practical requirements of Christianity would be impracticable and absurd without it. While, therefore, the foolishly wise discover matter of scorn in this view of religion, to the wisely foolish it exhibits the *wisdom* as well as the power of God, and gives harmony to the whole analogy of faith. History has demonstrated that the forms of Christianity may exist, in general vogue, among a community whose actual condition is hardly above that of the heathen: that it may advance, almost to perfection, the civilization of a people, with scarcely any improvement of their morals; and in every such state of society it will be found that the purely spiritual traits of Christianity, those that particularly belong to experimental theology, are lost sight of. This was the case at the period of the origin of Methodism. Read Wesley's own testimony made to the age. He says: "A total ignorance of God is univeral among us. The exceptions are exceeding few, whether among the learned or unlearned. High and low, cobblers, tinkers, hackney coachmen, men and maid servants, soldiers, sailors, tradesmen of all ranks, lawyers, physicians, gentlemen, lords, are as ignorant of the true God as Mohammedans or pagans."

The chief reason for that great moral deterioration which followed the restoration of the Stuarts was the absence of the fundamental principles of experimental Christianity in the church. The vital doctrines of the Reformation were almost entirely omitted from the popular inculcation of religion. These doctrines are inwrought into the very texture of the national Liturgy; they were enunciated in its beautiful service weekly, and in many places daily.

They had consoled, in the fires of martyrdom, the fathers of the English Church; but they had become sounds without significance. They were not distinctly exhibited in the preaching of the day, and the devotions of the desk were counteracted by the discourses of the pulpit. The ignorance of the clergy in the knowledge of their profession was incredible, if we can receive Burnet's evidence.

Some of the best theologians of the English Church existed during the period under review; but they were exceptions to the general character of the ministry. The theological student cannot but observe the difference between the writings of even such men as Waterland, Bull and Tillotson, on the one hand, and the Homilies, the wholesome evangelic productions of the reformers, Cranmer, Ridley, Latimer, and Jewel, on the other. Whitefield published a sermon on regeneration, which called forth numerous replies, all of which show that, however explicit the doctrine may be in the standards of the church, it was not known experimentally, nor theoretically, by many of the clergy. One of these declares "that, to tell Christians they must be born again, who, in the soundest sense, were born again [i. e. baptized] in their infancy, is, to say the least, a great impropriety."

"The church supposes they have already been born again, and she does not command them to be baptized, or born again, a second time." These are assertions from a "fellow of Clare-hall, Cambridge." A sermon was published by Dr. Stebbing, chaplain in ordinary to the king, against Whitefield, in which he endeavors to prove that regeneration is but another word for "the new man," and the latter but a figurative name of "practical righteousness." This sermon was indorsed and sent to Whitefield by the bishop of Gloucester. In his reply to the bishop's letter he justly says that the author "seems to know nothing more of the true nature of regeneration than Nicodemus did when he came to Jesus by night." The bishop of London, (Gibson,) in a pastoral letter, accused the Methodists of "professing to plant and propagate a new gospel, unknown to the generality of ministers and people in a Christian country." The charge referred to justification by faith, and no doubt the bishop's testimony can be relied on, that it was "unknown to the generality of ministers and people." Indeed, many of the leading prelates of the day entered the lists against Wesley and Whitefield, and most of them opposed the very doctrines which are now received as vital in the Christian sys-

tem. "Gibson compromised the apostolic doctrine of regeneration; Lavington caricatured it, Smallbroke all but denied the work of the Spirit, and Warburton evaporated divine influence."*
To the reformers of Oxford, therefore, the Christian world owes, in a great measure, the revival of those cardinal truths which the church has subsequently distinguished as pre-eminent, by calling them evangelical. It was the vitality of these truths that rendered so efficacious their ministry, and that still quickens all evangelical Christendom. Being the apostolic *doctrines*, they reproduced the apostolic *spirit*, and, since the date of Methodism, the primitive idea of missions has reappeared. Indeed, nearly all the plans of Christian enterprise, which now engage the attention of the church, have been adopted since. The Bible, the Sunday school, the tract, the temperance societies, as well as the principal missionary schemes of the church, have subsequently arisen. I do not assume that we owe them directly to Wesley, but that they sprung from the revival of the vital doctrines of Christianity: that Wesley was the leading agent in this revival, and Methodism its organized form.

Salvation, *free, full, immediate*, attainable by

* Philip's Life of Whitefield.

all, and experimentally *known,* these are the substance of Methodist theology. They are wholesome doctrines, and very full of comfort; blessed be God that we know them, and are commissioned to spread them through our sinful and sorrowful world. Let us preach, and emphasize, and reiterate these truths; they are full of gracious efficacy; the common sense of men will recognize them as the appropriate tenets of God's word, and their anxious spirits will find in them repose. Some of us have the impression that our special work is done; that other evangelical churches have become revived; and have so far adopted our views of experimental religion as that we need no longer feel the peculiar responsibility for the spread of these views, which devolved upon our fathers. Would that it were so; but we fear that it is far otherwise. We acknowledge that they have generally approximated our standard, but they have not yet reached it. They believe more than formerly in spiritual confidence and a higher standard of piety; but in how many of their vestry meetings can you hear the laity declaring their assurance that "the Spirit itself beareth witness with their spirits that they are the children of God," or that the blood of Christ "cleanseth them from all unrighteousness?"

In Methodist prayer meetings these are the perpetual topics; in other churches they are scarcely matters of allusion. Two of what we consider vital truths of religion are yet almost peculiar to us, namely, the *witness of the Spirit*, and *Christian perfection*. While we lament that they are not received by other churches, let us rejoice that they are household sentiments among ourselves, and bear in mind that on us devolves the responsibility of spreading them. While these views are peculiar to Methodism, it will be a peculiar privilege to be a Methodist, and those who owe to the Methodist Church their conversion, and yet join other communions, from the impression that all are now alike evangelical, mistake seriously. The late Dr. Fisk, though, while in a backslidden state, strongly inclined to the Protestant Episcopal Church, felt, when he received the blessing of "perfect love," the precious privilege of membership in a church where this doctrine was taught. "O, my brother," he writes, "I could write pages on this subject, but I must forbear. I thank God that I ever saw this day. I love our church better than ever. How glad am I that I never left it, and how thankful that they never cast me off when backslidden from the cause!"—*Life*, p. 73.

THE PRAYING MOTHER.

'He heareth the prayer of the righteous."—Solomon.

Mrs. L. is a remnant of the first generation of Methodists in B. She is still wending her heavenward pilgrimage, after many years of trial and change. Her husband was a sea captain, of French origin, a Catholic in his earlier religious education, but a decided skeptic in his maturer years, tolerating, with affability, the religious opinions of others, but utterly reckless of his own.

Mrs. L. consecrated her house to God; she erected the family altar and guarded its hallowed fire with the fidelity of a vestal priestess. Even her infidel husband was compelled to admire her Christian integrity, and during his stay at home, as well as his absence on the seas, she faithfully gathered her little ones in daily domestic worship. Skeptic as he was, he felt that that family altar shed a cheering and hallowed light on his hearth-stones, that it was a moral mooring to his household during his frequent and long absence—an affecting, though, it might be, an illusive reminiscence of their early home to his children, when, in after years, they might be dispersed in the world. Nay, often, in foreign ports, amid the dissipated scenes of a sailor's life, did strange and affecting images of that home worship, the supplications and tears of his wife and little ones for their wandering father, pass over his memory, and often, in the perilous extremity of the night storm, did the trembling unbeliever bethink himself that the evening prayer had gone up from affectionate hearts for him, and that good might it be with him if there should be a God to hear it.

Home, how salutary are its memories when sanctified by virtue! How do its dear images—the faces of sisters and brothers, fathers and mothers, though long since in the grave—follow the wanderer over the world, like the presence of blessed angels, ever and anon revealing themselves to his view as they hover over him with looks of sweet complacency or tender rebuke! Melancholy is the privation of those who have no such ministering memories, the record of whose homes, written on the heart, is only of estrangement and sorrow.

Mrs. L. believed not only in the moral influence of domestic religion, but in the direct answer, sooner or later, of her prayers in behalf of her husband and children. Years passed away without the realization of her hopes; but she persevered, humbly and hopefully, at her altar, till God answered her, though in a way she could not have anticipated. He blessed her by misfortune. She had occasion to correct her son one day by confining him to his chamber. The boy escaped by a window, and could not be found. Days passed away, weeks and months elapsed, and no intimation of the missing child was heard. The mother, wrung with anguish, still clung to the domestic altar. Misgivings, painful misgivings, met her there during these anxious months. Had she not had reason to expect a different effect on her children from her efforts in their religious education? Had God disregarded her supplications? Was it in vain that she planned and prayed, and wept before him for them? Ah! who has not had such assaults of the adversary in dark hours? But "trust in the Lord, and wait patiently for him." Know ye not that adverse providences are God's most common means of blessing? that he has led the church through the world, and his individual saints up to heaven in triumph, by them? Her boy was wandering, she knew not where; but God's providence was following him, and leading him to his salvation.

He had embarked in a vessel, and after a long voyage arrived in Charleston, South Carolina

Here he remained, destitute and dependent, several weeks; but at the moment of his extremity his father arrived unexpectedly in the harbor, from Havre, France. The boy, subdued by reflection and sorrow, flew to the arms of his parent, confessing his misconduct with tears. The juvenile romance of adventure had died in his bosom, but the tender remembrance of his home still lived, melting his young heart, and disposing him to return to its deserted altar, and mingle there his tears with those of a mother's anxiety and love

The vessel sailed for Havana. It arrived at a time when the yellow fever raged in the city. In a few days the poor boy, predisposed perhaps by his anxieties and grief, was attacked by the dreadful malady. And now revived, in overpowering force, the recollections of his early religious instructions. The confused reveries of a fevered brain could not dispel them. The atonement, the duty of repentance and faith, the terrors of death, judgment, and hell, were ever present to his mind. Ah! even in this extremity the prayers of the desolate mother were prevailing in heaven.

One day, when all hope of his recovery had gone, the father, a man of strong feelings, entered, with a broken spirit, the chamber where he lay. The dying boy, with his tears dropping upon the pillow, was sobbing the name of his mother: "My mother! my dear mother! O, that she were here to pray for me as she used to!"

The father bent over him, unable, for a time, to speak, but mingling his tears with those of his son. Clasping his trembling hands, and casting a look of appalling earnestness at his parent, the boy exclaimed, "Father, I am dying with my sins upon me! I shall be lost in my present state! Send, O send for some one to pray for me!"

"My child," replied the father, trembling with emotion, "there are none but Catholic clergymen on the island, and they cannot help you."

"O, what shall I do, then, father?" exclaimed the son.

"Pray for yourself, my dear child," replied the father, unwilling to repose the destiny of his son on his own infidel views of the future.

"I do," replied the boy; "but I need the help of others; O, can you not, will you not, pray yourself for your perishing son, father?"

The captain felt as if the earth shook beneath him. He had never prayed in his life: but his heart melted over his child; he felt, as by consciousness, the necessity and truth of religion. He felt that none but a God could meet this terrible emergency of man. As if smitten down, he fell on his knees by the bedside of his son. His spirit was broken; his tears flowed like rain, and, with agony, he called upon God to save himself and his child. The family and servants of the house were amazed; but he prayed on, and before he rose, his child's prayers were heard, if not his own. The suffering boy had found the peace which passeth understanding.

He died trusting in his Saviour, and full of tranquil hope.

Oppressed with sorrow, the father did not cease to pray for himself; he was deeply convicted of sin, and before long found peace in believing.

He returned to B—; his child a corpse, but himself a new man—the one in heaven, and the other on the way. He brought to his wife the first news she had received of her missing son. She wept; but with tears of gratitude as well as sorrow, acknowledging that, in affliction, God had blessed her. Her prayers had not failed. Providence had overruled the misconduct of her child for his own and his father's salvation.

Captain L. lived several years after this incient, a devoted Christian, and died praising God aloud for his mercy to him at Cuba.

The impressions of childhood, how ineffaceable are they! How, amid the confusion and dissipation of later life, do they still abide, though concealed—like burning coals, smothered, but not extinguished, amid the rubbish that afterward they consume! Search the records of Christian biography, especially of the Christian ministry, and you will find that a striking proportion were the children of Christian parents, or, at least, of Christian mothers. If there are any prayers which, more than others, must prevail with God, they are those of the devoted mother pleading for her wandering child.

THE JEWS.

"My covenant will I not break."—Psalmist.

No people, whose annals have ever had a record in the history of the world, afford so many anomalous peculiarities as the Jews. Their history is a wonderful record of almighty providences. Descending from a single man, a venerable patriarch, and friend of God, they were multiplied like the stars of heaven, and the sands on the seashore; and from a national infancy, spent in bondage, they were led by the hand of a parental Providence through every vicissitude of national elevation and depression. At one time, guided by the Almighty in a symbolic cloud and burning pillar, they triumph over their foes, and spread the fear of their name among the nations; at another, they mourn in captivity, and hang their harps on the willows of a strange land. Once their holy city rises in splendor, with its glorious temple dignified by the attendance of monarchs, and sanctified by the services of inspired prophets and priests; and now, the ploughshare is driven through its foundations, their whole national organization broken up, their population, like the stars of heaven scattered over the firmament, dispersed to the boundaries of the world.

And yet this singular and inscrutable course of events, in the national history of the Jews, was described beforehand, in prophecy, with almost the same minuteness with which time itself has developed it.

By Moses it was written: "The Lord shall scatter thee among all people, from the one end of the earth even to the other; and among these nations shalt thou find no ease, neither shall the sole of thy foot rest; and thou shalt become an astonishment, a proverb, and a by-word, among all nations whither the Lord shall lead thee; and thou shalt be only oppressed and crushed alway." But yet, with all these afflictions, the Jews were to be preserved. "Yet, for all that, when they be in the land of their enemies I will not cast them away, neither will I abhor them to destroy them utterly." "I will make a full end of all the nations whither I have driven thee, but I will not make a full end of thee."

What a literal history, written three thousand years before the events, was this of the present condition of the Jews!

1. They were to be "scattered among all people, from one end of the earth to the other."

2. They were to find no ease nor rest to the sole of their feet.

3. They were to be persecuted with reproach: "an astonishment, and a proverb, and a by-word."

4. But not cut off: "I will not cast them away, neither will I abhor them to destroy them utterly." This prophecy, in all these respects is now in actual exemplification on the face of the whole world.

Here we have a living and everywhere existing monument of the truth of prophecy—a perpetuated miracle, the laws of nature suspended, and the analogy of things interrupted.

While all the other nations of the ancient world have lost their national identity, and either faded from the earth or been merged in new combinations, the history of this singular people presents us with the anomaly, as observed by an able writer, not merely of a river, which, after rising from its small mountain spring, continues to flow through the ocean of waters without mingling with the general mass, but the more striking prodigy of one whose waters have become dispersed through the whole extent, and, by the vicissitudes of the tides, carried to every tributary stream, and yet each drop retaining its distinctiveness from the mass, and prepared at any time to be collected together. What, but a most special Providence, has enabled this singular race to resist all the social affinities that mix and connect men in society; and, with a dispersion co-extensive with the earth, under all climes, in all latitudes, in all longitudes, among all nations and kindreds, and tongues and people, maintain their national character without a national organization? Bowed down with afflictions, oppressed by the legal institutions of almost every country under heaven, and where the civil constitution of society does not grind them down, yet failing to remove the doom of Heaven, the instinctive repugnance of mankind humbles them to the ignominy of an inferior and despicable caste; rejected of God, outcast of men, it seems as if the stars of heaven fought against them in their courses. The sun, in his career, has been hailed in every clime by their cry of lamentation and wo, as if the hand of divine judgment held them up to the gaze and scorn of the revolving world, and yet made them immortal in dissolution itself.

The prophecy states, that though God should make "a full end of all the nations whither he would disperse the Jews, yet of them he would not make an end." This has been fulfilled. The nations that were contemporary with them in the days of their national existence live only in the narration of the historian, or the desolate vestiges that tell to the passing traveler the sites where stood their walls and towers. Babylon, Nineveh, and Tyre, have all passed away from the list of nations. The descendants of their ancient inhabitants are lost in the mass of the world's population. But the sons of Israel still retain their ancient character, preserving uncorrupted their lineage from the patriarchs, the prophets, and warriors of their sacred times; they travel, though "with weary foot and restless breast," yet still the sons of ancient Zion, over the ruins of the nations within whose once mighty walls their fathers were led captive in chains, and whose present condition their prophets proclaimed in the ears of trembling monarchs. Though accursed, they stand up, in all the world, witnesses for the God they offend. In the ends of the earth, in the isles of the sea, in the cities of Asia, Europe, and America, on the Alps and the Himalaya, on the Alleghanies, the Cordilleras, and the Andes, they wander among the nations, yet remain distinct.

In the past and present peculiarities of this afflicted people we have a certain pledge of the fulfillment of the prophecies which declare their future conversion and restoration. Though dispersed over the extent of the earth, and diffused through the whole mass of its population, yet, from the distinctness and identity of their character, they are prepared, at any time, to obey the call of that Almighty voice which has announced to the nations that the time of their deliverance is yet to come. And for what purpose have they been kept a distinct people, but that they may yet be restored to the favor of God, and reinstated in their ancient and holy land? Where is the infidel speculator who can read this lesson of Providence, and dare deny its convincing clearness?

AN INCIDENT WITH A LESSON.

"The Lord lifteth up the meek."—David.

There is moral strength in meekness—it is among the surest evidences of sincerity, and this, itself, is a mighty means of influence. But there is, also, in its very aspect and tones an intrinsic power, a suitableness to conciliate and affect the mind. "A soft answer," says the wise man, "turneth away wrath." "I am meek and lowly in heart," said the incarnated Almighty. When accompanied by superior abilities what an effectiveness does it impart to them! Artists tell us that contrasts heighten effect. Splendid abilities put forth with meekness and humility appear but the more commanding—they take us by surprise. A person with such traits conciliates us by his character while he controls us by his powers; and, where no superior talents are possessed, humility is a grace beautiful, because befitting. The Rev. Mr. R——, in a sermon before a numerous audience, composed in part of preachers, related an interesting anecdote, illustrative of the influence of humility in subduing a suspicious and repugnant mind. He was urging the ministers present to humble perseverance in their labors, notwithstanding their peculiar trials, assuring them that success would attend them often where they least expected it. A young preacher, said he, on going to a distant field of labor, had occasion to stop over night with a farmer, a member of a Calvinistic church, an honest man, but, unhappily, of a peevish, suspicious temper, that had been exasperated by several instances of imposture, in which vagrant men had availed themselves of his hospitality under the character of Christian ministers. The young preacher had just commenced his ministerial career, his appearance was not prepossessing, and he was depressed with anxieties respecting his untried field of labor.

It was late in the evening when he reached the gate of the farm-yard. The farmer came forth to meet him, but with chilling coldness. He made surly inquiries about his name, whence he came, whither he was going, etc., expressing, meanwhile, by looks, his suspicions; and giving very direct intimations about false pretensions, etc. Weary and depressed as was the stranger, he felt a momentary indignation, but, repressing it, he resolved to copy the meekness of his Master, and, by his example, if not otherwise, attempt to curb the perversity of his rustic host. He was pointed to the stable, with permission to feed his horse, and come into the house. As he approached the house he was directed to the kitchen. Some food was spread upon a rude table for him. The hired men in .he kitchen whispered to each other their surprise that he was not invited into the parlor. Though of humble origin himself, he felt keenly the indignity of his treatment; the pride of his heart for a moment revolted, and he arose to resume his journey, with the prospect of a rainy night; but he suddenly checked his feelings, and, looking to God, resolved to await patiently the result of this strange scene.

It was not long before all were called into another room for family prayers. The preacher followed the hired laborers, and took his seat in a corner. The farmer read a chapter in the Bible. At the end of it he was evidently embarrassed by an inward struggle, not knowing what to do; but, finally, turning to the preacher, he abruptly asked him to pray. They knelt down, and the young man, oppressed with feelings which prayer could best relieve, poured out his soul and tears before God. A divine influence came down upon all present; they sobbed around him. The meek pathos of his tones, the spirituality of his sentiments, the evangelical views involved in the prayer, and its prevailing earnestness, struck all present. The morose farmer, subdued and melted, approached him at the conclusion of the prayer, and, in the presence of the family, with flowing tears, begged his pardon.

"I should not have been so suspicious," he said, "but I have been all day under a strong temptation of the adversary—my mind has been irritable—my conduct toward you to-night is a mystery to myself—I cannot account for it even by the state of my mind during the day. I have not been myself or I would not have so treated you. Forgive me, sir. How have you been able to endure it?"

"My Lord," replied the youthful preacher, "has said, Learn of me, for I am meek and lowly in heart. It is my ambition to do so. Try, my brother, to learn the same lesson." It was the keenest rebuke that could be given to the farmer; he felt its pertinency, made the humblest acknowledgments, and begged his maltreated guest to tarry at the house several days, and preach to the family and neighbors. His engagements would not allow him to remain so long; but, such was the importunity of his host, that he consented to preach the next day. That night he reposed in the best chamber of the house and his rest was sweetened by the thought that he had conquered a perverse mind by an example of meekness. The next day he preached with deep effect, and went on his journey with the prayers and blessings of the farmer.

"And what," said the Rev. Mr. R——, "do you suppose was the result? The old farmer was a better man ever after; the sermon of the young preacher had a salutary influence on the whole neighborhood, several were awakened, and among these three of the farmer's children; two of them have since gone safe to heaven. Ah! it is the temper of Christ that fits us for usefulness!"

During the relation of this anecdote, the Rev. Mr. C., who was one of the hearers, was deeply excited. His color changed frequently, and, at the conclusion, he burst into tears, and was so overpowered and faint that he had to be led out. On recovering his strength and self-possession, the mystery was solved. He was the young man alluded to by the preacher, but he had never learned before the happy results of the circumstance. When the preacher mentioned them he was taken by surprise; grateful joy filled and overflowed his heart, and his emotions were too intense for his strength.

"Cast thy bread upon the waters, for thou shalt find it after many days."

METHODISM—ITS SPECIAL CHARACTER.

"Wesleyan Methodism is one of the greatest developments of Christianity during the last century."
Rev. R. S. Chandlish, Edinburgh.

It is all important to the continued prosperity of Methodism that its friends ever bear in mind the special character of its mission. *Methodism is a special system, and every Methodist ought to be a special Christian.* Titus ii, 14. Its whole history and character are impressed with the marks of a special design. It originated at a special time, a period in which, as we have seen, Dr. Watts declared that "religion was dying in the world;" and when Butler assures us that Christianity was "treated as if it had, at length, been discovered to be fictitious." "Just at the time," says Wesley, " when we wanted little of filling up the measure of our iniquities, did two or three of the clergymen of the Church of England begin vehemently to call sinners to repentance." Few periods in the history of the English Church were darker. I have already shown that natural religion had become the substance of preaching; that Arianism and Socinianism, under the influence of such men as Priestley, Whiston, and Dr. S. Clarke, were current among the learned; that the most giant advocates of skepticism England has produced —Hobbes, Bolingbroke, Hume, and Gibbon— were appearing, or just had appeared, in the conflict with Christianity; while, across the channel, the strong-holds of the Reformation were yielding to a deistical theology, and the French philosophers were spreading moral contagion through Europe. At this dark period did God raise up Wesley, Whitefield, and their co-laborers, and thrust them out to revive the elementary doctrines of Christianity, and exemplify again the apostolic spirit and labors.

Not only did it arise at a *special time*, but the *men who introduced it were special men*. It is not hazarding much to say that, in the group of its earlier characters, we meet with some who were the most extraordinary in their respective spheres that have appeared since the foundation of Christianity:—Wesley, one of the greatest of ecclesiastical legislators; Whitefield, the most extraordinary pulpit orator; Charles Wesley, the best of sacred poets; Fletcher, one of the most profound polemics; Coke, the greatest leader of modern missions; Asbury, the most laborious of bishops; and two commentators, Clarke and Benson, one among the most learned, and the other among the best of practical expositors. Who can doubt the evidence of divine Providence displayed in the coexistence and co-operation of these remarkable men ?. While Wesley was employing his wonderful powers in constructing and establishing the economy of Methodism, Whitefield was rousing for it the popular sympathies by his eloquence, and preparing especially other sects for the influence which time has shown it was destined to exert upon them; Charles Wesley was imbodying its tenets and spirit in verse, and preparing, for its future hundreds of thousands, an unrivaled psalmody; Fletcher was defending, with a battle-ax which nothing could withstand, its theology, and vindicating it as much by his spirit as his logic; Coke was developing its plans of foreign conquest; Asbury, the great pioneer of American revivals, was applying its energies to the new circumstances of this continent; and Benson and Clarke followed, fortifying it firmly on the foundation of the Scriptures. These were the leaders; but the subordinate instruments were likewise marked by strong characteristics, distinguishing them as men raised up by God for an extraordinary purpose.

The *measures* of Methodism bear the same special character. Dr. Chalmers has characterized it as "Christianity in earnest." Effect, and *immediate* effect, is its uniform intent. Wesley and his coadjutors preached the common doctrines of the gospel, but distinguished them more clearly, and emphasized them more strongly, than others, insomuch that they struck the public attention as new truths. They were not content with the limits of church edifices, but betook themselves to the open air. Stationary labors could not satisfy their zeal; but they went up and down the land, preaching by night and by day; they "ran to and fro, and knowledge increased." Methodism could not delay its great designs by waiting for a ministry qualified by the old course of preparatory education; but revived the apostolic example of a *lay ministry*. It could not allow these the limited labors of a single charge; but hastening them from place to place, it revived the means by which the apostolic ministry conquered the world—an *itinerant ministry*. Not content with its regular labors, it appropriated all its subordinate energies in the new offices of *local preachers*, *exhorters*, and *leaders*. While it retained the more formal means of grace, it either introduced, or adopted, the *class-meeting*, the *band-meeting*, the *prayer-meeting*, the *camp-meeting*, the *love-feast*, and the *watch-night*.

Thus it studied to apply every energy, and to apply it in the most productive manner. The effective system of American Methodism exemplifies well this, its practical energy. It is a vast and powerful machinery. Our general conferences, annual conferences, quarterly conferences, leaders'-meetings, and class-meetings; our gradations of labor—bishops, presiding elders, circuit preachers, stationed preachers, local preachers, exhorters, and leaders—form a series of instrumentalities unequaled in the economy of any other Protestant denomination.

Not only has it been thus special in the circumstances of its origin, in its characters and measures, but also in its *spirit*. What candid observer, however he may question some of its peculiarities, will deny, that a more than common share of the divine influence has been vouchsafed to it, and that its system has been extraordinarily productive? We assert it, not boastfully, though gratefully, and as an *unquestionable fact of its history*—a fact which ought to be particularly regarded, if we would appreciate the system and mission which God has appointed us. How is it, otherwise, that such general and constant revivals prevail under it? that so many thousands have been rescued by it from the lowest conditions of vice? that such multitudes have passed from within its pale joyfully to the church triumphant? and that a number, exceeding, by nearly one half, the next largest sect in the land, are still marching under its banners to the same heavenly Jerusalem? This special success is the result of a special energy, and all men, whose eyes are open, behold it.

Methodism is essentially vital and operative: it must ever be so: *it is an absolute necessity of its system.* And herein we observe a peculiarity which ought to strike, most impressively, its friends as guarantying, with the divine blessing, its perpetual integrity and prevalence. All other sectarian forms of Christianity have declined. Congregationalism, with its simple rites, became a lifeless system of religious commonplaces. "Protestant Episcopalianism" degenerated into a spiritless ritual. All the distinctive and essential traits of each have coexisted with a general absence of vital religion. The state of the English Church when Methodism began was an example of the latter; the state of the New-England Church before and after Edwards of the former. But we can hardly conceive of Methodism in such a state. While these denominations have lost their vitality, without losing any of their distinctive traits, *Methodism abso* lutely cannot thus decline without the extinction of all that is distinctively Methodistic in its system. We are almost induced, in this view, to consider it a final form of Christianity—a millennial system. How can we conceive of a lifeless laity imbodied in classes, and meeting weekly to converse of Christian experience? Or of a dead ministry, leading the pilgrim life of itinerants? Or of such a laity hearing, and such a ministry preaching, the distinctive doctrines of Methodism—*distinguishable conversion, the witness of the Spirit, and Christian perfection?* Herein, then, is Methodism unique: it cannot, like other sects, decline seriously, and retain its distinctive character: it can only fall by a *revolution* of its whole practical system: it must lose its identity, and be no longer Methodism. We do not assert its infallibility, but its singular security. It may experience such a revolution; but who will predict it?

In all these respects Methodism is marked with a special character and a special purpose. Wesley said that its purpose was to "spread holiness over the land:" but it is greater: it is o "spread holiness over the world." It was raised up, not merely to resuscitate the English Church, but to affect all Protestant Christendom, either by its direct action, or by its exam-

2

ple. *It is a missionary church in its plans, a revival church in its spirit;* and such it promises to be until the world is redeemed.

I have said that it is important that we bear in mind the special character of our cause.

First, the idea of our special character will lead us to *bear patiently the special inconveniences of our system.* The greatest of these, to both people and preachers, arise from our *itinerancy;* and the most serious objection under which our polity suffers is brought against the *appointing power* upon which the itinerancy is based; yet this itinerancy, with its episcopal basis, is the most indispensable feature of our economy. Abolish it, and you cut the locks from your young giant. Besides its moral effect upon the ministry, by reminding them that here they have no abiding city; and upon the people, by the constant distribution of our various talents, it is necessary to the support of a large portion of our appointments. Many of these do not afford a full support to the preacher; and thus it must be while there is a frontier to our work; and such a frontier there must be till the world is evangelized. Some of them require actual suffering. Methodist preachers are of like passions with other men: they know it, and therefore have they adopted a system which, by its authoritativeness, will not allow of the indulgences and evasions of selfishness; and, by the frequent changes which it effects, distributes and relieves the inconveniences which it imposes. What would become of these indigent appointments, if the appointing power were vested in the whole conference, or a committee of its appointment, subject to an appeal to the conference? Who would appoint himself to such posts? Who would not feel disposed to escape, by all possible means, the embarrassments and sufferings which most of our preachers now endure? Some there might be, who, brave of heart, would court perils, and exult in the brunt of the battle; but many, without doubt, would seek, like troops in the field, who should have the choice of their own position, the securer posts. I have no doubt that one-third of all our appointments would be left unsupported in a few years after such a revolution in our ecclesiastical polity. I do not depreciate our preachers by this remark; I base it on a just view of human nature; all who understand human nature will accede to it. Their work is *militant:* like men in battle, they know they must suffer, must stand amid mortifications and perils, which are rarely matters of voluntary choice; and, therefore, like soldiers, in the emergencies of war, they pledge themselves to obey their leaders; but those leaders are of their own constitution, and the measure of obedience is of their own devising. Selecting the fathers of the ministry for their superintendents, they say unto them, "Here we have no abiding city," and, "Though bonds and afflictions await us, yet none of these things move us; neither count we our lives dear unto us, so that we might finish our course with joy, and the ministry which we have received of the Lord Jesus, to testify the gospel of the grace of God:" point us, therefore, to the positions most suitable for us; let them be easy or perilous, secure or dangerous, "here are we; send us."

This is the language of a genuine Methodist preacher; and this is not the language of servility, but of a heroic spirit of self-sacrifice, produced, under God, by that truly militant system which some, indisposed to its labors, or impatient of its authority, would abolish. Let it be abolished, and the permanent triumphs of Methodism cease: our ministry will become like other ministries. What other preachers go, or would go, where Methodist preachers go? With all their poverty and illiteracy, are they not the front line of the American ministry on the borders of civilization? and do they not, in our older communities, perform labors and sustain burdens which few, if any, of the clergy of other sects do? And how but by the peculiarity of their system?

Let it not be objected that the English Methodist preachers are subject to no such absolute control. If it were true, yet there is no analogy between the cases. There is no English preacher who does not get a comfortable support, either from his people or the funds of the conference. The English Conference receives no appointment except as a mission, unless it can support a preacher. The appointments of the English preachers are made by a committee. This is virtually the case in the American church, the presiding elders being to all intents and purposes, such a committee in conjunction with the bishops; and, for my own part, I would rather have such a committee, composed of men who, from their official position, can have a knowledge of the general demands of the work, and are not liable to the interferences of personal interest, than one composed of men who have a common place with myself in the list of appointments. The English preachers were subject to an individual and absolute appointing power, until about the time in which their fiscal system allowed of a modification; and the appointments of this committee are generally as inexorable as those of our committee of presiding elders and bishops. Indeed, a large majority of Wesleyan preachers have no voice whatever in the proceedings of their conference. But one hundred can act at all, as instituted by Wesley.

We believe Methodist preachers are almost universally and immovably attached to their present government. A few aspiring or disappointed spirits may revolt, a few more of better integrity may, for want of a close investigation of its advantages, wish for a change; but the latter generally come out right in the end; and the former have never permanently injured us, and have never been succeeded by the providence of God. Meanwhile Methodism is advancing in triumph. Tens of thousands flock to her ranks yearly, hundreds of thousands have gone up to heaven from her pale, and hundreds of thousands are on their way. They have been opposed at each inch of their advancement, but they have pressed onward, and from all quarters the cry is, Still they come! In the village and in the city, in the wigwam of the savage and the hut of the slave, on the shores of the Puritans and on the banks of the Columbia, amid the colds of Canada and the savannas of Texas, the preachers of this "despotic" system are suffering and triumphing. On them and on their fields God has deigned the greatest outpourings of his Spirit in modern times; and there is but one prospect before them, if they will preserve, unimpaired by innovation, their economy and doctrines, and that is, universal progress.

Second, it will explain *the indisposition of the church to change its polity*, by conforming it to the notions of those who clamor for what they call a republican church. There are theocratic traits of the Christian church, which will not allow fully of such a character. The most ostensible department of the church—the ministry—is not representative; it cannot be created, though it should be sanctioned, by the people: God alone, by the election of his Spirit, can appoint men to preach; and such as he calls are the divinely-authorized expositors of his truth and administrators of evangelical ordinances and discipline. The question of religious liberty pertains not so much to the church as to the state. Where the civil government imposes no religious system, the rights of conscience are guarantied. Under its broad shelter men may properly form the most rigorous religious combinations, provided they can enter into and retire from them voluntarily.

The appointing power of the Methodist episcopacy I have shown to be one of the most essential features of our polity: when it is abolished our itineracy will become a nullity. And yet this is the peculiarity of our system which is most abhorred by "reformers," so called. And why this hostility to it? Is not its chief pressure on the ministry; and is it not a creation of the ministry itself? Our bishops do not usurp this high prerogative, but the ministry itself maintains it, and appoints the bishop to bear it. The ministry can repeal it, if it pleases. Why, then, this outcry against an authority which is voluntarily sustained by those who suffer its chief inconveniences? Is it said that "such a prerogative involves undue power? It is inconsistent with the republican principles of the country?" etc. I reply, that it is not more so than some usages which the civil policy of our country creates and sanctions. The country sustains an army. The power of military command is absolute, even unto death. The soldier's only maxim in the field is, "Obey," if it carries him to the mouth of the cannon. And yet, he is a free citizen of this republican government, in all his civil relations. I men tion this case merely to show the absurdity of that indiscriminate cry of "republicanism," "personal rights," etc., which is so unceasingly uttered by reformers. I love republicanism: my attachment to it grows with my growth; but I love it too much to see it abused to the purposes of anarchy. By the sweeping generalizations of such logicians, we must not only abolish our military and naval regimen, but also the government of our colleges and academies, and of most of our voluntary organizations. There is no leading denomination in the land whose system is strictly modeled after that of the civil government. The Methodist community are as true to their country as any other sect; but they have found their religious economy peculiarly successful. It was not devised, but grew up providentially; and, being assured of the protection of their individual rights by the civil law, they have not deemed it wise to risk its efficiency by attempting to adjust it to the relative and abstract rights of its different subjects; but consent to a mutual sacrifice for the common good. Their only object being the "spread of holiness," their only inquiry is, "How shall we most effectually accomplish it?"

Third, *the influence of this single impression will be powerful.* Let it be the universal idea of the church that we may lead on the aggressive movements of Christianity, and our zeal will be redoubled. Hitherto we have been surprised at our own success, without a definite inference of its future results. We have exclaimed, "What hath God wrought!" and wondered whereunto it would tend. Standing now far in front of the religious bodies of this great nation, and prominent in the van of those of Europe, we ought to project plans for the future; and they should be sublime ones, befitting the gospel, and comprehensive as our lost world. Our zeal should look forward to the time when Methodist itinerants shall traverse the wilds of Africa and the deserts of Tartary, and shout for joy along the Andes and the Himalaya. "But this is enthusiasm:" yes, it is; yet it does not transcend the power or the promise of God. It is the enthusiasm that inflamed the prophets and bled on the cross for our redemption; and it must yet thrill through the church before she will put on her full energy. Heretofore she has moved by occasional impulses. Ever and anon a glory, as of the latter day, has dawned upon her, but been followed by darkness. But now good men are looking at the signs of the moral heavens with new eagerness and hope. In al. lands great and effectual doors are opening

New means of spiritual warfare are constantly arising. A special providence seems to control the course of civil events. The political arm of antichrist at least is broken, and the crescent of the false prophet but gleams on the horizon. Great revivals are waking up Christendom; and the idea is becoming general in the church that the morning of the latter day is upon us, and the final battles are at hand. In these circumstances, how stands Methodism? One of the largest corps of the evangelical host, disciplined and hardy by nearly a century of conflicts, possessing energies unequaled by any other sect, and lacking only a more definite conception of its true capability to enable it to scatter dismay and trembling among the powers of darkness. We have a tolerable idea of the nature of our mission, but not of its extent. We work well at the posts which have fallen to us, but show a culpable hesitancy in assuming our true position. Denominations of much less strength are before us in their efforts for education, missions, etc., and their influence on the public mind. Being first in numerical strength, it devolves on us to be first in all Christian efforts; but we are not yet second. Our missionary contributions are an example: our present income would be quadrupled by each member paying only a cent a week. Let the idea of our special mission be generally received, and it will at once arouse us from this apathy; and, when once awakened, we shall find our resources a hundred-fold greater than we have apprehended them to be. O that the young generation of Methodists, to whom is committed the future, may understand their " high calling," and " acquit themselves like men!". Let them be admonished that theirs will be a rare responsibility, and, if faithfully sustained, as glorious in honor and reward as in responsibility

VISIT TO THE TOMB OF WHITEFIELD.

"Mighty through God."—Paul.

In a late journey through New-England, I stopped at Newburyport to see the tomb of Whitefield. The visit will always be memorable to me. It suggested reflections impressive and profitable. Whitefield's name belongs to Methodism; his partial separation from Wesley was a misfortune, but his life was spent in the same great evangelical movement. We must not forget that he belonged to the "Oxford Club;" that he was the first of the little band that carried the true light into the coal mines of Kingswood, and the first who had the courage to preach in the open air. His stirring eloquence prepared the popular mind for the more systematic operations of Methodism in both England and America.

His remains are deposited in a vault under the Federal-street church—a church in which he had often preached, and in sight of the house in which he expired. As we passed near the altar our attention was arrested by a massive marble cenotaph, erected to his memory by a wealthy gentleman of the town. The sexton, having lighted his lantern, led us into a little vestry behind the pulpit, in the floor of which is a small trap-door. This he opened, and we descended into a dark apartment, much like a common cellar. On one side of this apartment is a door opening into the vault, which extends under the pulpit. We passed into it. The faint light of our lantern gave a solemn gloom to this dark but hallowed resting-place of the great modern evangelist. Three coffins lay before us; two containing the remains of ancient pastors of the church. The lid of each was open sufficiently to show the head and chest, and the skeleton faces stared on us with ghastly expression, as we held over them our dim light. Our footsteps and our subdued voices called forth a faint and trembling echo, and even this tomb of glorified saints seemed instinct with the gloom and dread of death, reminding us of the doom of the fall.

A slight depth of black mold covered the bottom of Whitefield's coffin, and on this lay the bare bones. I took his skull into my hands, and examined it with intense interest. What thoughts of grandeur and power had emanated from that abode of the mind, and stirred with emotions the souls of hundreds of thousands —emotions which will quicken their immortality! I held it in silence, but my mind ran over the history of the " seraphic man ;" and started, and endeavored to solve, a thousand queries respecting the attributes of his character, and the means of his wonderful power My reflections followed me from the place. I asked myself what constituted the peculiar efficiency of Whitefield's preaching?

Doubtless, the first, the strongest cause of it, was that remarkable combination of the unction from above, the "Holy Ghost and power," with intense natural sensibility, which distinguished him. He was "full of faith and the Holy Ghost." In him religion was from the time of his conversion to his death a continual impulse; zeal for souls an unbroken spell. All his theological opinions, his ideas of sin and holiness, of heaven and hell, were not merely *thoughts*, but *sentiments;* not speculations, but unquestionable realities. They were appreciated by him as vividly as sensible facts are by ordinary men. This vivid spirituality inflamed his entire soul, and made him pass through the churches like an angel of light. A spiritual unction seemed to drip down his whole person, like the anointing oil that " went down to the skirts of Aaron's garments."

It has been said that all his sentiments were passions. Few, if any, ever had keener sensibilities. Remarkably strong affections characterized the whole course of his life. "While seeking religion," he says, "God only knows how many sleepless nights I have lain on my bed, groaning under what I felt. Whole days and weeks have I spent lying prostrate on the ground in silent or vocal prayer." It was the working of his strong sensibility that gave a charm to his preaching, and drew, as by magic, the multitudes after him. Under his first sermon, it was reported that "fifteen persons were driven mad," that is, convicted of sin. His popularity was immediate and boundless. Speaking of one place, he says, "The whole city seemed alarmed, and the doctrine of the new-birth made its way like lightning into the consciences of the hearers." On visiting Bristol, multitudes came out of the city on foot and in coaches to escort him; and the people hailed him as he passed through the streets. His congregations were so crowded that he could with difficulty make his way to the pulpit. "Some hung upon the rails of the organ-loft, others climbed upon the leads of the church, and, altogether, made the church so hot with their breath, that the steam would fall from the pillars like drops of rain." Sometimes, after his preaching, the multitude, little children and old men, went weeping and wailing through the streets.

When he visited Scotland the second time, the people crowded to the shore at Leith, weeping and blessing him; they pursued his coach to Edinburgh, pressing to welcome him when he alighted, and to hold him in their arms. "The effect which he produced," says a distinguished writer, "was maddening." At Cambuslang it was incredible. He says, "I preached, at two, to a vast body of people, and at six in the evening, and again at nine. Such a commotion surely never was heard of, especially at eleven at night. For about an hour and a half there was such weeping, so many falling into deep distress, and expressing it in various ways, as is incredible. The people seem to be slain by scores. They are carried off, and come into the house like soldiers wounded in and carried off a field of battle. Their cries and agonies are exceedingly affecting. Mr. M. preached, after I had ended, till past one in the morning, and then could scarcely persuade them to retire; all night, in the fields, might be heard the voice of prayer and praise." On returning to administer the sacrament, he says, "Scarce ever was such a sight seen in Scotland. There were upward of twenty thousand persons. Two tents were set, and the holy sacrament was administered in the field. When I began to serve at one of the tables, the power of God was felt by numbers; but the people crowded upon me so that I was compelled to desist, and go and preach at one of the tents while the ministers served the rest of the tables. On Monday morning I preached again to near as many; such a universal stir I never saw before. The emotion fled as swift as lightning from one end of the auditory to the other. You might have seen thousands bathed in tears, some at the same time wringing their hands, others almost swooning, and others crying out and moaning over a pierced Saviour." The cool-headed Scotch divines, unaccustomed to such scenes, wrote a pamphlet to prove they were diabolical, and a day of fasting was actually appointed for his being in Scotland. Such powers of discourse were, perhaps, never before witnessed. An ignorant man once characterized his eloquence aptly, when he said, "Mr. Whitefield preached like a lion."

It was, I repeat, this prevalence of mighty feelings, the result of divine grace and natural sensibility, that chiefly constituted his eloquence. He *felt*, and the speaker who feels will make his hearers feel, whatever may be his other deficiencies.

Secondly, he had not only the soul of eloquence, but also the art. Elocution is not eloquence. A speaker may be eloquent without it: he may have it in perfection, and not be eloquent. But Whitefield, while possessing the moral and intellectual elements of the orator neglected not the practical principles of the art. It is said that he studied and privately practiced the precise rules of public speaking. His gestures are said to have been remarkably appropriate; those who heard him often, say that each repetition of the same sermon showed a studied improvement, and that several repetitions were necessary to perfect its effect. His voice was laboriously cultivated, and became astonishingly effective. Garrick, who delighted to hear him, said that he could make his audience weep or tremble merely by varying his pronunciation of the word Mesopotamia.

In the third place, his style, both of language and address, was natural—it perfectly comported with his strong natural feeling. Though he studied the art of eloquence, he was not artificial. The ornate, the florid style, so commonly received in our day as eloquence, was utterly absent in Whitefield. No one, studying his genius, can conceive, for a moment, that it was possible for him to use it. He was too much in earnest, too intent on the object before him

His language is always simple and colloquial, not fitted for books, but, therefore, the better fitted for speech, abounding in abrupt transitions, and strongly idiomatic—such language as a sincere man would use in earnestly entreating his neighbor to escape some impending harm. Though he did not like his reported sermons, they are evidently fac-similes of his style—direct, abrupt, full of local allusion, and presenting scarcely a single ornamented passage—the very speech of the common people. It would appear homely, even meager, did not the reader supply, in his imagination, the conversational manner, the tears, and the entreating voice of the speaker. Here is an example, taken at random:—

"But, say you, all in good time; I do not choose to be converted yet. Why, what age are you now? I will come down to a pretty moderate age: suppose you are fourteen; and you do not think it time to be converted? and yet there are a great many here, I dare say, twenty years old, and not converted. Some are of opinion, that most people that are converted, are so before thirty. There was a young man buried last night at Tottenham Court but seventeen, an early monument of free grace! Are you forty, or fifty? Is not that time? Is it time for the poor prisoners to be converted that are to be hanged to-morrow morning? If it is time for them, it is time for you, for you may be dead before them. There was a poor woman, but two or three days ago, that was damning and cursing most shockingly; now she is a dead corpse; was taken suddenly, and died away. God grant that may not be the case with any of you; the only way to prevent it is, to be enabled to think that *now is an accepted time, that now is the day of salvation.* Let me look round, and what do you suppose I was thinking? Why, that it is a mercy we have not been in hell a thousand times. How many are there in hell that used to say, Lord, convert me, but not now? One of the good old Puritans says, hell is paved with good intentions. Now can you blame me, can you blame the ministers of Christ, if this is the case? Can you blame us for calling after you, for spending and being spent for your souls? It is easy for you to come to hear the gospel, but you do not know what nights and days we have; what pangs in our hearts, and *how we travail in birth till Jesus Christ be formed in your souls.* Men, brethren, and fathers, hearken, God help you, save, save, *save yourselves from an untoward generation.* To-night somebody sits up with the prisoners; if they find any of them asleep, or no sign of their being awake, they knock and call, and the keepers cry, Awake! and I have heard that the present ordinary sits up with them all the night before their execution; therefore, don't be angry with me if I knock at your doors, and cry, Poor sinners, awake! awake. and God help thee to take care thou dost not sleep in an unconverted state to-night. The court is just sitting, the executioner stands ready, and before to-morrow, long before to-morrow, Jesus may say of some of you, *Bind him hand and foot.* The prisoners to-morrow will have their hands tied behind them, their thumb-strings must be put on, and their fetters knocked off; they must be tied fast to the cart, the cap put over their faces, and the dreadful signal given: if you were their relations would not you weep? don't be angry, then, with a poor minister for weeping over them that will not weep for themselves. If you laugh at me, I know Jesus smiles. I cannot force a cry when I will; the Lord Jesus Christ be praised, *I am free from the blood of you all:* if you are damned for want of conversion, remember you are not damned for want of warning. Thousands that have not the gospel preached to them, may say, Lord, we never heard what conversion is; but you are gospel-proof; and if there is any deeper place in hell than other, God will order a gospel-despising Methodist to be put there. You will have dreadful torments; to whom much is given, much will be required. How dreadful to have minister after minister, preacher after preacher, say *Lord God, I preached, but they would not hear*. Think of this, professors, and God make you possessors!"

Such a mode of address, fraught with the emotions of Whitefield, could not but interest a popular audience. How does it contrast with the polished phrases and formal mannerism of tho pulpit generally! Who could go to sleep addressed in this direct style? Who could divert his attention from the subject to think of the speaker? I do not say that a more refined style is not appropriate to the pulpit; but, let its refinement be what it may, it should have these characteristics of simplicity, point, and colloquial directness. This is the style of true eloquence; ornament pertains to imagination, and imagination belongs to poetry; but poetry and oratory are distinct. Genuine oratory is too earnest to admit of much ornament. Its figures are few, and always brief. Its language is the language of the passions, not of the fancy, and the passions never utter themselves in embel-

lished phrases, but always directly, pungently
The great mistake of modern oratory, especially
in the pulpit, is, that we have confounded it
with poetry.

THE CHRISTIAN USE OF MONEY, WITH EXAMPLES.

"Ye cannot serve God and mammon."—Christ.

WE plan incessantly for the pecuniary interests of religion, and yet how little comparatively is done! Where is the fault? Doubtless systems and agents are requisite; but the great difficulty to be surmounted is, after all, that stern and common-place one, the selfishness of the human heart. Hence the ever-reiterated assaults of the Scriptures on " covetousness. which is *idolatry*." I wish to record a word on the subject, and would to God it might be a forcible one.

The proper use of money by Christian men is a question without any definite shape to most minds. Wesley's sermon on it is seldom read among us, and everywhere apparently disregarded. Now and then a remarkably pure minded Christian, like Cobb, Goodell, &c.

catches the true idea of the New Testament respecting it; but, alas! how few feel that they are "bought with a price, and are not their own!" Many of the Christian poor do feel this sentiment, and live in accordance with it, for their temptations to feel otherwise are not strong; but such is the perverting influence of prosperity that its exemplification among the rich is an anomaly neither demanded nor expected by the church. And yet, Christian reader, those rigorous sentences of the New Testament on the use and dangers of money *are stern and abiding truths.* Heaven and earth may pass away, but one jot or one tittle will not pass from them. They may be forgotten, or depreciated, as insignificant commonplaces now; but they will flame out on the books of final judgment, and you will stand or fall by them for ever. Every accumulating dollar is with you either an instrument of good or a sinking weight. Are you, then, prospering, are you laying up treasure upon earth— you, the redeemed child of Him who had not where to lay his head, and who, though he was rich, yet for your sake became poor? Pause, then, and examine your stewardship. Perhaps you are old and descending to your grave, and yet, through years of accumulation, have not once examined this point, or estimated how much could be spared from your just wants for the cause of God. Would to God that this word of warning could arrest you a moment and direct your thoughts intently on the question. A thousand paltry suggestions are now doubtless trying to divert you from it; but O! permit them not; think, think this once on the subject, and remember, while thinking, that, on your right and on your left, before you and behind you, millions are sinking into eternal death—millions whom your Lord redeemed by the blood and agony through which you have hope!

Do you ask, What would you have me do? I answer, Be more *definite* in your contributions to the cause of God. Investigate thoroughly your affairs, and ascertain how much is requisite as the capital of your business when prudently conducted, and there, in the fear of God, fix an inexorable limit to it—from its annual income deduct what is requisite for your temperate livelihood and the education of your children, consecrate the rest to God, and at death leave a suitable part of the capital to your children, to be used in a like manner for their subsistence and the good of the world. What! must I do so if it is several thousands a year? Yes, if it is several hundred thousands. Shrink not at this. A worldling, without the love of man and the hope of heaven, may shrink; but you are an "heir of glory:"—

> "Yonder's your house and portion fair,
> Your treasure and your heart are there,
> And your abiding home;"

and in your pilgrimage thither you linger here only to procure and use the means of salvation for others. Alas! how have you utterly forgotten the use of these means, and hoarded them while the world has been perishing! The blood of souls may stain your hands, Christian brother; haste and wash it away. Would you retain your treasures for the happiness they may procure? O heed me! I can tell you of happiness, the purest in this world, which may be purchased by them—*it is the happiness of knowing that they are all consecrated to God.* This consciousness will sweeten your days and irradiate your nights. Are you old? it will restore the gladness of your youth: are you sinking with declining health? it will accompany you, like an angel of bliss, into the grave: are you young? it will shed sunlight over your coming years.

Names have been referred to which are examples of the course here recommended. In a late publication a writer mentions a case not the less noble for being humble. He says:—

"Meeting with a pious young mechanic, who had lately read the 'Memoir of Normand Smith,' he spoke to this effect:—'Several years I have given about one-fourth of the profits of my calling to charitable purposes, and have merely saved enough to keep my little family above want, should I be called away by death; and so soon as I reach that point, instead of giving one-fourth, I will give all my profits, and thus follow Normand Smith as he followed Christ; for I fully accord with the sentiment expressed in his Memoir.'"

This is an example for the mechanic and the poor. The passage in Mr. Smith's Memoir referred to is so pertinent that I cannot forbear quoting it:—

"In regard to pursuing business with the view of getting property to be used for the Lord, a volume ought to be written on this subject. Christian men of business do by no means feel its importance as they ought. At a time like this, when funds are so much needed to send the gospel through the world, I see not why young men of enterprise and piety may not and ought not to devote themselves to business for the sole purpose of accumulating means to carry forward the benevolent operations of the day. There are some who now act on this principle. The number ought to be greatly increased. There ought to be missionary tradesmen and merchants just as much as missionary schoolmasters and preachers—men prosecuting business for the great purpose of getting to give into the treasury of the Lord. Nor can there be a doubt that all who should act on this principle would lay up, both for themselves and their families, not only a *good*, but the *best*, foundation for a time of need. It has been thought by some that Mr. Smith went beyond the demands of Christian duty in giving so large a portion of his property to benevolent purposes. Of this he was certainly the rightful judge. Having made what he deemed a competent provision for his wife and children, he felt that what remained was the Lord's, and to him he gave it: and though the selfish may wonder, and the wealthy deem it injudicious, the unrolled records of eternity, I cannot doubt, will show that he acted with the soundest Christian discretion—that he did what was best for his family, as well as what was right and pleasing to his divine Lord. His fatherless children have a better portion than of silver and gold, and their prospects of happi ness, here and hereafter, are far greater than if they had been left heirs, each, to an estate of tens of thousands."

We have a striking example also in the history of Solomon Goodell, of Vermont. He was truly one of God's noblemen, and is no hyperbolical model for all Christian men of business. Jeremiah Evarts, himself one of the excellent of the earth, has recorded some facts in his history which I condense.

His property could not, at any time, have been sold for five thousand dollars, but he pursued a course of charity, *as a business of life*, with a laborious self-denial, and an enlarged catholicism, which unitedly formed a character of Christian heroism, as rare as it is honorable.

About the year 1800 Mr. Evarts observed a donation of one hundred dollars to the Connecticut Missionary Society, published in the annual accounts as from Mr. Goodell. Such donations were, at that time, very uncommon in this country, and in regard to that society nearly or quite unprecedented. The thought occurred, that, doubtless, some gentleman of independent fortune had taken up his residence in the interior of Vermont, and that he considered the society a good chanel for his beneficence. This conclusion was strengthened by seeing a similar donation from the same source, at the return of each successive year for a considerable period.

When the American Board of Foreign Missions began its operations, Mr. Goodell did not wait for an agent to visit him, but sent a message (or came himself) more than fifty miles, to a member of the board, saying that he wished to subscribe five hundred dollars for immediate use, and one thousand dollars for the permanent fund. He sent fifty dollars as earnest money, and said he would forward the remaining four hundred and fifty dollars as soon as he could raise that sum; and would pay the interest annually upon the one thousand dollars, till the principal should be paid. This engagement he punctually complied with, paying the interest, and, just before his death, transferring notes and bonds secured by mortgages, which (including the one thousand dollars above mentioned) amounted to one thousand seven hundred and eight dollars and thirty-seven cents; that is, a new donation was made of seven hundred and eight dollars and thirty-seven cents, to which was afterward added another bond and mortgage of three hundred and fifty dollars.

Mr. Goodell had made what he thought suitable provision for his children, as they passed through life. After consulting his wife, he left her such a portion of his estate as was satisfactory to her, gave several small legacies, and made the board his residuary legatee.

On visiting Mr. Goodell at his house, you would find no gentleman with an independent fortune; but a plain man, in moderate circumstances, on one of the rudest spots in the neighborhood of the Green Mountains, every dollar of whose property was either gained by severe personal labor, or saved by strict frugality, or received as interest on small sums lent to his neighbors. His house was comfortable; but, with the farm on which it stood, was worth only between seven hundred and a thousand dollars. His income was derived principally from a dairy.

We have a most interesting example in the case of Mr. Cobb. The following statements are condensed from a sketch published by the American Baptist Publication Society:—

Mr. Cobb resolved at the commencement of his religious life that he would serve the Saviour, with all his power, in that sphere which seemed particularly assigned to him. God endowed him with peculiar talents for business, so that he acquired property with great rapidity; and, if he had chosen to devote himself to the narrow work of amassing wealth, he might perhaps, if he had lived, have become a rival of Gerard. But he had justly regarded his talent for business as an instrument which he ought to employ for the glory of his Saviour. He felt it to be his duty to use it in earning money for the cause of God, on precisely the same principle that it is the duty of the minister to devote his talents for preaching to the service of the Lord Jesus. He accordingly, in November, 1821, drew up and subscribed the following very remarkable document:—

"By the grace of God I will never be worth more than fifty thousand dollars.

"By the grace of God I will give one-fourth the net profits of my business to charitable and religious uses.

"If I am ever worth twenty thousand dollars, I will give one half of my net profits; and if I am ever worth thirty thousand dollars, I will give three-fourths, and the whole after fifty thousand dollars. So help me God, or give to a more faithful steward, and set me aside."

To this covenant he adhered with conscientious fidelity. He distributed the profits of his business with an increasing ratio from year to year, till he had reached the point which he had fixed as the limit of his property, and then he gave to *the cause of God all the money which he earned.* At one time, finding that his property had increased beyond fifty thousand dollars, he at once devoted the surplus, seven thousand five hundred dollars, as a foundation for a professorship in the Newton Theological Institution, to which he gave, during his life, at least twice that sum. So scrupulous was he in his adherence to the covenant which he had made, that when peculiar circumstances required him to retain in his possession more than fifty thousand dollars, he consulted judicious friends whether he might do so consistently with the spirit of his pledge, provided he always held the surplus as really belonging to the cause of God. Here is the secret of that wonderful liberality which cheered so many hearts, and gave vigor to so many institutions and plans of benevolence. It sprung from steady religious principles: it was the fruit of the Holy Spirit. He always felt that God had bestowed on him a rich blessing, in enabling him to serve his cause. On his death bed he said to a friend, in allusion to the resolutions quoted above, " By the grace of God—*nothing else*—by the grace of God, I have been enabled, under the influence of those resolutions, to give away more than forty thousand dollars. How good the Lord has been to me!"

But Mr. Cobb did not wait till he had acquired fifty thousand dollars, before he began to devote his money to religious uses. While he was yet young, and comparatively a poor man, recently established in business, he resolved to give one-fourth of the net proceeds of his business to benevolent purposes. It was then uncertain what would be his success; but he felt it to be his duty to begin then, with the resolution to increase the proportion if God should prosper him. Some Christians say they must first make provision for themselves and their families, and then they will distribute their money liberally. Mr. Cobb did not act thus. He, from the beginning, gave a large proportion of his income, and trusted in God that whatever should be necessary for himself and his family would be supplied.

I have spoken emphatically on this subject, but not too strongly, for here is the root of the whole matter. *We have no definite principles of duty in our charities;* some give liberally, but it is casually. Before the church will be fitted for its great mission, its business men must be brought to consider their business relations to God as strictly as they do those which regard men, their accounts must be daily cast up with reference to the judgment day, and her youth must be trained to the above principles. I know not how to dismiss the subject. There are some reading these lines to whom they are applicable; happy, thrice happy, would the writer be if he knew what argument to adduce, what words to use, by which to impress indelibly their minds. Again, Christian brother, you are entreated not to evade this appeal. It is made to you—made in the name of your Redeemer and your perishing race. If it has never been made to you before, it is now made, however feebly. If you drop this volume and go into the world resuming your usual indifference, remember, O remember, that your forgetfulness cannot destroy the inexorable obligations of duty, and that the impressions of this hour, though forgotten, will revive when the dead awake.

2

BISHOP ROBERTS.

"The voice of one crying in the wilderness."—Matthew.

I HAVE received this evening the melancholy intelligence of Bishop Roberts' death. Many a labor-worn veteran of the itinerancy will weep as the sorrowful news spreads; for he was beloved among us as an old commander is among the troops whom he has led to battle and victory.

A score of reminiscences of the sainted old man revive in my memory: his dignified bearing, his white locks, his noble brow, his mild blue eye—the most benignant I ever saw—his tranquil temper, which I never saw ruffled, his extreme modesty, his exquisite delicacy of feeling so singularly combined with the hardy *bon hommie* of the backwoodsman; and, above all, the unction of his piety. Ah, he was a man to be loved while living and to be remembered pathetically when dead—the St. John of our apostleship!

Bishop Roberts had no one trait which, by extraordinary prominence, gave him uniqueness, or what is usually called greatness. The distinction and beauty of his character was its equability. I doubt if he ever felt a quarter of an hour's irritation since the day of his conversion. A symmetrical mind is truly great, though seldom so appreciated; it is at once rare and capable. It is what is most requisite, next to holiness, for the high office which the bishop sustained in the church, and his election to it was owing in a great measure to the estimation in which his judicious constituents held this qualification. It was perceived and valued in him by the older preachers, and especially by Asbury, at his first appearance among them, at the Baltimore General Conference of 1808. He had traveled to Baltimore, from the then western wilds, with bread and provender in his saddle-bags, and but one dollar in his pocket. He appeared before them in rude guise and unpretending humility, but was immediately appreciated by the preachers and people, and was soon after transferred by the sagacious Asbury to that city. In a few years he was appointed to Philadelphia; from the city station he was raised to the presiding eldership of the district; and it was in that city, while presiding in the annual conference, in the absence of a bishop, that his equanimity, his calm and discriminating judgment, and other corresponding qualifications, suggested his nomination to the episcopacy. The next month he was elected bishop, at Baltimore. I have always looked upon his election as providential. The great field of Methodism was to be the west. It was then rapidly opening; and Roberts was the man for the west. He was a child of the wilderness; he had been educated to its hardy habits; his rugged frame and characteristic qualities, all designated him as a great evangelist for the great west. Though born in Maryland, he was removed in early childhood to a wilderness part of Pennsylvania, then on the border of civilization. Here he spent his youth in the labors of the "settler." When the region began to be extensively settled, he pushed forward with a few brave pioneers into Chenango, at that time public land offered as a bonus to emigrants. There he built his log cabin, and dwelt comparatively out of sight of civilized man, tilling the earth in summer, and hunting the bear, the deer, and the racoon, in winter. He became one of the most expert huntsmen of his day, and, in after life, often surprised veteran marksmen, on the far frontier, by the deadly certainty of his fire. The entire winter has he spent at his solitary log cabin, twenty miles away from any human habitation, and cheered only by the faithful company of his favorite sister, who prepared his repasts of wild meat.

The refinements of the Atlantic cities could not repress the ruling passion of his youth—it followed him through life, and was strong even in death—he lived a circuit preacher as he had a "settler," and a bishop as he had a circuit preacher, in a *log cabin;* and died in a log cabin. No sooner had he been elected a bishop than he fixed his episcopal residence in the old cabin at Chenango; and his next removal was to Indiana, then the far west, where his episcopal palace was a log cabin built by his own hands, and his furniture rude fabrications from the forest wood, made with such tools as he had carried in his emigrant wagon. I have been authentically informed, that the first meal of the sainted bishop and his family in this new abode consisted only of roasted potatoes, and that it was begun and ended with hearty thanksgiving. Here he lived in the true simplicity of frontier life, toiling, at his leisure, in the fields. The allowance for his family expenses, besides two hundred per annum for quarterage, was, during most of his episcopal career, from two hundred to two hundred and fifty dollars per annum; at least this was the case till 1836. Such is the pomp of the Methodist episcopacy!

Simple and severe as this western life was, it was legitimate to the character and position of Roberts. He was born unto it; it comported with the new field, the great wilderness diocese of the Mississippi Valley, into which he was thrust. There was in it a propriety with the genius of the country, with the *tout ensemble* of the circumstances of time and place. Such was the life for such a field; and Roberts was the man for both such a field and such a life. Let us learn to follow providence in all things; there is always a beautiful compatibility between its ends and its agents. The history of our church is full of such examples.

This congeniality of the bishop's character with western life attracted about him the strong affections of the western preachers. They felt that he was legitimately one among them. In his latter years they venerated and loved him as the patriarch of the wilderness. His visit to the last Missouri Conference, as described in our papers at the time, was an example. He had spent some months before in a most laborious visitation among the Indian missions beyond Arkansas and Missouri. His health was evidently undermined by years and toils; and the time of his departure was at hand. The preachers looked upon him as peculiarly their own bishop—their father; and, while trembling with infirmities, he addressed them, at the reading of the appointments, in the crowded court-house of Jefferson city : they wept aloud, invoking, in audible ejaculations, blessings on the old evangelist. He had presided at their first conference, more than a quarter of a century before, when it included nearly a third of the great Mississippi Valley, and had attended more than half its sessions since : but three or four of its original members remained : he made thrilling allusions to the old preachers who had gone up to their reward ; and gave much information respecting the progress of their work. As he alluded to his own health, and the little prospect of ever meeting them again in this world, his voice faltered, he paused, and they all wept together like the elders of Ephesus when taking leave of Paul. "I feel," said the bishop, "like a father leaving his children"—words that went to the hearts of all present, and called forth tears and irrepressible sobs from preachers and spectators. It was his final leave—in about six months he ascended to heaven.

As usual with equable minds, Bishop Roberts was cheerful and amiable. His piety was never gloomy, though seldom ecstatic. You felt at the first introduction that he must be one of the most agreeable companions ; that he could calmly endure afflictions, and compassionately forgive offenses ; that he was fitted for domestic life and permanent friendships.

As is natural with such a disposition, he was generous and liberal. I have heard of numerous examples of his benevolence from the best authority. Those who knew well his private affairs have estimated that his pecuniary contributions, during his ministerial life, amounted to more than all his receipts from the church for domestic expenses. He was especially liberal to our literary institutions. He prized learning from a sense of his own deficiency in it, having had but about three months' instruction after his seventh year. To four of our colleges he gave, at intervals, one hundred dollars each. In 1826, when in New-Orleans, he found the brethren attempting, with few resources, to erect a cheap church ; he sold his horse, and, giving them all it brought—a hundred dollars—made his way with many difficulties to Nashville, where his friends provided him with a horse and funds with which to finish his journey. While at home, in the periods between his episcopal visitations, he labored hard in the fields, that he might have the means of indulging this noble propensity of his generous mind. He was as whole-hearted in his labors. According to his routes, the last year he lived, he must have traveled between five and six thousand miles, visiting some half dozen states and nearly an equal number of Indian nations.

As a preacher he was always interesting, and frequently eloquent. His passions never had undue play in the pulpit. A thoroughly systematic arrangement of his subject, readiness of thought, fluent, and generally correct diction, and a facile yet dignified manner, were his characteristics in the desk. His large person—corpulent, and nearly six feet in height—his strongly-marked features—elevated forehead—and manners of extreme simplicity and cordiality, gave to his presence always the air of a superior man—one to be remembered and loved.

It is certainly no small tribute to his character to say that its greatest apparent defect was the excess of a very amiable quality—he was constitutionally modest. In his earlier life this disposition rendered him painfully diffident and throughout his career it deterred him from many bold and energetic measures, which his position and abilities justified, and which might have been of wide influence on the church. He often referred facetiously to instances of his early diffidence. For a long time after his appointment as class-leader, among his rustic neighbors, he could not assume courage enough to address them individually, and he had actually to be superseded by another leader till he conquered this timidity. In his first attempt at public exhortation, he suddenly sat down appalled at the intent look of a good man whose favorable interest he took for disapprobation. At another time, when he was expected to exhort, he was so alarmed as to retire in agony and conceal himself in a barn. In the third attempt he proceeded some time with good effect, but, fearing he had made a blunder, stopped short in confusion.

In after years this extreme diffidence became a subdued modesty, not interfering with his ordinary duties, but deterring him from most novel or experimental plans, however hopeful, and leading often to ludicrous mistakes among those who did not know him. When stopping in his travels among strangers, he usually assumed no other pretensions than those of a private Christian; and frequently it was not till the family worship declared his spirit and talents that his ministerial character was supposed. Under such circumstances he has sometimes attended class-meeting with his host, and received warm and pointed exhortations from zealous class-leaders. On returning to the west, after a

General Conference, he once applied at the house of a Methodist family to which he had been recommended for entertainment. He was as usual humble in dress, and dusty and weary. The family, taking him to be a rustic traveler, permitted him to put up and feed his horse, and take his seat in the sitting-room. Supper was over, and no one took the trouble to inquire if he had taken any on the way. The preacher of the circuit was stopping at the same house—he was young, frivolous, and foppish—and spent the evening in gay conversation with the daughters of the family, alluding occasionally and contemptuously to the "old man," who sat silently in a corner. The good bishop, after sitting a long time, with no other attention than these allusions, respectfully requested to be shown to bed. The chamber was over the sitting-room, and, while upon his knees praying with paternal feeling for the faithless young preacher, he still heard the gay jest and rude laugh. At last the family retired without domestic worship. The young preacher slept in the same room with the bishop. He laid down without prayer.

"Well, old man," said he, as he got into bed, "are you asleep yet?"

"I am not, sir," replied the bishop.

" Where have you come from ?"

" From east of the mountains."

" From east of the mountains, aye—wha place ?"

" Baltimore, sir."

" Baltimore, aye—the seat of our General Conference—did you hear anything about it ? We expect Bishop Roberts to stop here on his way home."

" Yes, sir," replied the bishop, humbly, " it ended before I left."

" Did you ever see Bishop Roberts ?"

" Yes, sir, often ; we left Baltimore together."

" *You* left Baltimore together ?"

" Yes, sir."

" What's your name, my old friend ?"

" Roberts, sir."

" Roberts ! Roberts ! Excuse me, sir, are you related to the bishop ?"

" 'They usually call me Bishop Roberts, sir."

" Bishop Roberts ! Bishop Roberts ! are you Bishop Roberts, sir?" said the young man, leaping out of bed, and trembling with agitation.

Embarrassed and confounded, he implored the good man's pardon, insisted upon calling up the family, and seemed willing to do anything to redeem himself. The bishop gave him an affectionate admonition, which he promised with tears never to forget; acknowledging, at the same time, that he had backslidden in heart, and deeply lamenting his folly and his spiritual declension. The venerable and compassionate man knew the frivolity of youth; he gave him much paternal advice, and prayed with him. He would not allow the family to be called, though he had eaten nothing since breakfast. The next morning, after praying again with the spirit-broken young preacher, he left before the family had risen, that he might save them a mortifying explanation.

The circumstance was a salutary lesson to the young itinerant; at the next session of the —— Conference, he called upon the bishop a renewed man; he wept again as he acknowledged his error, and has since become a useful and eminent minister. Bishop Roberts often alluded to the incident, but, through a commendable kindness, would never tell the name of the young preacher.* Other and similarly ludicrous rencounters might be mentioned.

* This fact has been extensively circulated, with some exaggeration, and with Bishop George substituted for Bishop Roberts. Bishop Roberts was its real subject.

Peace to the memory of the good, the kind hearted old man! His image is embalmed in the affections of many a heart, and will there be enshrined faithfully through future years of pilgrimage and change. He has passed to the society of his old co-laborers. May we who love his memory join him there!

HERETICAL TENDENCIES OF METHODISM AND CALVINISM.

"I will also show mine opinion."—Job's friend

I HAVE just been reading in a Calvinistic paper a singular charge against Methodism. It alledges, in substance, that Methodism tends to laxity in religion; that "affecting proof" of this tendency is seen in the numerous additions made to Universalist churches from among Methodists, and that as Arminianism once led the New-England churches to Unitarianism, so it is now, in connection with Methodism, leading to Universalism.

Now it may be confidently asserted that there is neither fact nor logic to sustain this novel charge. The history of Methodism is altogether against it. I do not doubt that there have been individual cases of apostasy from Methodism to Universalism; but they are not characteristic of the body; they are not more frequent among Methodists than among most other evangelical sects. I believe I have some acquaintance with Methodism, but am unable now to recall one instance. Such there may have been, and, perhaps, in some few places in considerable numbers, so as to form the nuclei of

Universalist societies; but I have never heard of them. I know not a single Methodist chapel perverted to the use of Universalists. But, is it not a well-known fact, that such apostasies from Calvinism have been frequent; and that not a few Calvinistic houses are now in the hands of the Universalists? For every one derived from the Methodists, five can be referred to which were once Calvinistic, especially in New-England, where Universalism succeeds best: there the facts are known and read of all men.

Nor is there logic in this charge. It would seem that our Calvinistic brethren cannot dissociate the idea of religious laxity from Methodism. It arises from their confounding Methodism with European Arminianism. The latter is not Methodism. It has no sympathy with the Pelagian Arminianism of continental Europe. Its Arminianism consists in its denial of pre-reprobation and a limited atonement. But what, in the name of all logic, is there in this that tends to religious laxity? Is it necessary, for the purity of Christians, that they believe God has irretrievably, and from eternity, cast off most of the human race? There is a rigorous bigotry, sometimes taken for piety, which may be produced by such a sentiment—but never genuine piety. Methodism teaches the possibility of "falling from grace," and the necessity of "working out our salvation with fear and trembling." Does this savor of laxity? Calvinism teaches the final certainty of the salvation of the elect. Does this tend to spiritual strictness? Methodism has now been in operation more than a century. Where has one of its churches lapsed into Unitarianism? But have not nearly all the Unitarian churches of England and the north of Ireland sprung from Calvinistic Presbyterians; and, in New-England, from Calvinistic Congregationalists? And how is it on the continent of Europe? The strong-holds of Calvinism have nearly all become the intrenchments of Socinianism and Rationalism. In Geneva, the scene of Calvin's labors, there was not, in 1812, a single evangelical preacher. The pulpit in which he preached the "horribile decretum," as he calls it, is now occupied by a Socinian; and the theological school, where he lectured, is now used for the preparation of Deistical clergymen. The few Evangelists who have lately arisen in that city have revived the old dogmas; they will find them the chief obstructions to their success. Now what has caused these changes? The people of New-England know from local observation. It was the repulsive, the intolerable character of the old theology—not its experimental nor its practical, but its speculative character. The best sentiments of human nature revolted at its ideas of the divine government; and men in flying from one extreme passed to the other; in escaping from the desolate rocks of Scylla they plunged into the vortex of Charybdis. Arminianism is the safe position between the two extremes. In their transition they could not but cross it; *and hence Arminianism has been charged with the responsibility of their errors.* Arminianism is no more responsible for them than Calvinism is for the errors of the Mohammedans, who believe with Calvin in predestination.

The following three statements are not unworthy a little attention:—

1. Arminianism has almost always been combined with serious errors among those who have been repelled from Calvinism. But,

2. There is no one doctrine in Arminianism as preached by Methodists, which has a natural tendency to laxity in religion. It has less of this liability than Calvinism, logically compared, doctrine for doctrine.

3. During the very period that errors, connected with Arminianism, have been desolating the Presbyterian churches of old England, and

the Congregational of New-England, an Arminian organization has been growing, in these very countries, into immense strength and numbers, spreading itself out to the ends of the earth, and, in this land at least, exceeding, by nearly two-thirds, the combined numbers of the Congregational and Presbyterian Calvinists, until it has become the largest sect in these States, and with scarcely a defection of a pastor or church to those heresies which have raged in the former.

Which, then, is the cause of these heresies—Calvinism or Arminianism?

2

WESLEYAN ANECDOTES.

"*Marvelous things.*"—Psalmist.

YESTERDAY I spent a most agreeable afternoon with Rev. R. R., of the Wesleyan Conference, an excellent man, intelligent, refined, deeply evangelical, and sufficiently advanced in years to possess, in combination with mature experience and sound judgment, the mellow sentiments and cheerful temper of a ripe old age. He was one of the colaborers of Wesley, and abounds in most entertaining anecdotes of early Methodism. Now, it so happens that my humor runs in this current, and Mr. R.'s seemed perfectly to coalesce with it, so that the colloquial stream flowed rapidly and merrily. I put down snatches of the conversation.

He had witnessed some of the extraordinary physical effects of religious excitement which occur at our camp meetings, and remarked that they seldom appear now-a-days on the other side of the waters. Neither of us knew how to account for these anomalous circumstances except on some yet undiscovered law of the nervous system. They had at first puzzled Mr. Wesley much; he believed them to proceed sometimes from the devil, at others from divine influence; but in his later years, discouraged them decidedly. Mr. R. had witnessed these phenomena, at their first appearance, at Kingswood, and described them as altogether inexplicable. The stoutest men fell to the earth as suddenly as if shot through the heart; bold blasphemers were instantly seized with agony and cried aloud for mercy, and scores were sometimes strewed on the ground at once, insensible as dead men. A traveler, at one time, was passing by, but, on pausing a moment to hear the sermon, was directly smitten to the earth, and lay there apparently without life. A Quaker, who was admonishing the by-standers against these strange scenes, as affectation and hypocrisy, was himself struck down, as by an unseen hand, while the words of reproach were even upon his lips. A weaver, a great disliker of dissenters, fearing that the new excitement would alienate his neighbors from the church, went about zealously among them to prove that it was the work of Satan, and would endanger their souls. A new convert lent him one of Wesley's sermons; while reading it he suddenly turned pale, fell to the floor, and roared so mightily that the people ran into the house from the streets and found him sweating, weeping, and screaming in anguish.   *   *   *   *

2

Mr. R. referred with much interest to many of his old associates in the itinerancy. He had never heard a preacher superior to Samuel Bradburn. He was full of sublimity, mighty, grasping thoughts, and melting pathos, and yet mingled with the whole, in the strongest contrasts, an exhaustless wit. Dr. Coke, said Mr. R., used to declare that there was but one man whom he could hear preach longer than forty-five minutes, and he was Samuel Bradburn. A number of young preachers were speaking once rather whiningly of having given up *all* for the ministry. They put too much emphasis on their sacrifices, in Bradburn's estimation; he wished to rebuke them, and did it with his usual felicity. He had been a cobbler himself, as well as a tinker, and most of the young men in the company had been in equally humble occupations. "Yes, dear brethren," exclaimed he, "some of you have had to sacrifice your all for the itinerancy; but we old men have had our share of these trials. As for myself, I made a double sacrifice, for I gave up for the ministry two of the best *awls* in the kingdom—a great sacrifice truly to become an ambassador of God in the church and a gentleman in society!"

* * * * * * *

Mr. R. spoke with enthusiastic affection of his old friend, Gideon Ousley, the apostle of Methodism in Ireland. Ousley, said he, is one of the most eccentric of men, yet full of faith and the Holy Ghost. His mind is strong, and he has a university education. His family belong to the aristocracy, yet he became a Methodist itinerant, and has traveled the Irish highways, preaching the gospel, for more than twoscore years. He preaches everywhere—at cock-fights, horse-races, fairs, and markets, and hundreds of times has he proclaimed the gospel on horseback. His sermons are at least three a day, usually two in the open air and a third in a barn or meeting-house. He preaches often in the Irish language—a speech rich and powerful for exhortation. Ousley has rescued hundreds, perhaps thousands, of his countrymen from the superstitions of Popery. He has often been attacked by Popish persecutors, and lost one of his eyes in a scuffle with them; but though frequently beaten and left for dead, he is as bold as a lion, and scatters light among them at every point. Many of his persecutors have been overtaken by unnatural deaths, and the Papists dread him as protected by the devil When his uncle, Sir George Ousley, died, he inherited his wealth and title, but abandoned all, preferring the honor of being a Methodist itinerant above the estates and titles of nobility. Such a man is one of God's genuine noblemen.

* * * * * * *

I inquired of him particularly about Charles Wesley, of whom we have comparatively so little information that his position in Methodist history has always appeared to me vague if not ambiguous.* Charles Wesley, he replied, was a high-churchman: he could not appreciate the mission of Methodism. Much of his own ministerial conduct was in violation of his high-church opinions, for his good feelings could not yield to his prejudices. Yet Methodism owes much to him; he was the first of the brothers converted, and the first who received the appellation of Methodist. He stood by John till death, though dissenting from many of his measures.

Three elements prevailed in his mental constitution—*music, poetry, and faith.* He was all soul, from head to foot; full of vivid, though pensive, enthusiasm. He was an excellent musician: melody was sweeter to him than honey or the honey-comb; and his sons,

* Jackson's Life of Charles Wesley has been published since, one of the most entertaining and valuable memoirs in our biographical catalogue.

through his example, were prodigies in the art from their infancy. In the poetic art, who equals him among uninspired writers of the sacred lyric? He was incessantly expressing himself in poetry. He has touched the lips of all our hosts with live coals from off the heavenly altar, and will touch the lips of millions to come; but the hymns in our Hymn-book can afford no idea of the extent of his poetical compositions; they would fill volumes, and they uniformly possess his characteristic terseness and harmony. As is usual with poetic genius, he was subject to intervals of melancholy, and often so profoundly dejected as to long for the relief of the grave. His faith, however, kindled in the enthusiasm of his spirit, and aspired above his depressions. These three elements made him, as a man, most affectionate and generous; as a writer, always rhythmical and inspiring, and as a preacher, one of the most affecting and powerful in our history. He far excelled his brother in the unction and effect of his sermons. At times he became almost seraphic, and melted all hearts by the pathos of his feelings and tones. Such was Charles Wesley.

* * * * * * *

He spoke eloquently of Fletcher. John Fletcher is a name associated in my mind with every saintly quality. He was "the angel of the church." His temper was as felicitous as it was holy; religion illuminated his life like a perpetual sunshine. He was a living example of the spiritual doctrines of Methodism, as well as its controversial champion. Like the angel at the gate of paradise, he defended it with a flaming sword from the intrusion of error. He seems to have been providentially raised up to assist Wesley in the revival and defense of the apostolic doctrines. While the latter traversed the realm, publishing them, the former, with a polemical acumen seldom equaled, was defending them by his pen in his solitude at Madeley. His writings are an impregnable rampart around the theology of our church, and will endure while the church endures. Wesley said he was intimately acquainted with him for above thirty years; he conversed with him morning, noon, and night without reserve, during a journey of many hundred miles, and, in all that time, he never heard him speak one improper word, nor saw him do an improper action. In all the compass of his extensive acquaintance, he declared that he knew not one so devoted to God. And then his death—what a scene for the contemplation of angels! His joyous spirit grew holier with the lapse of each day, until it burst forth with triumphant raptures, and ascended, like a flame, to heaven.

* * * * * * *

Again the conversation ran off into the more striking scenes of early Methodism. Mr. R. related several remarkable cases of conversion. John Furz, one of my old associates, said he, was listening to one of our preachers, who exclaimed, "Two witnesses, dead and buried in dust, will rise up against you. These are they," holding up the Bible, "the two Testaments which have been buried in dust on your shelves." "I recollected," said John, "that my Bible was thus neglected, and that I had actually written my name with my finger upon the lid. I thought I had signed my own damnation on the back of the witness." He was horror struck—went home and called upon God for mercy, and lived and died a faithful preacher. John Thorpe, another old friend of mine, was converted in a still more singular manner. He and his comrades were one day ridiculing and mimicking the Methodists. They attempted to preach for a wager. John's turn came last: he mounted the table full of hilarity; but, on opening the Bible at the text, "Except ye repent ye shall all likewise perish," he was seized with terror; his hair stood on end, and he preached in earnest. At the close he ran home, called upon God in genuine repentance, and afterward went preaching through the land.

. . . . I have known of a tavern-keeper, who, relishing music, went to one of the meetings merely to hear the singing. He was afraid of the preaching, and, that he might not hear it, sat with his head inclined and his fingers in his ears. But a fly lit upon his nose, and, at the moment he attempted to drive it away with one of his hands, the preacher uttered, with power, the text, "He that hath ears to hear, let him hear." The word took hold upon his conscience, and he found no relief till he became a converted man. . . . In Wexford, Ireland, a conversion occurred still more odd. Our people were persecuted by the Papists, and met in a closed barn. One of the persecutors had agreed to conceal himself beforehand in the barn that he might open the door to them after the people were assembled. He crept into a sack hard by the door. The singing commenced; but the Hibernian was so taken with it that he thought he would hear it through before disturbing the meeting. At its conclusion he thought he would hear the prayer also; but this was too powerful for him; he was seized with distress and trembling, and bawled out with such dismay as to appal the congregation, who began to believe that the evil one himself was in the sack. The sack was at last pulled off of him, and discovered the poor Irishman a weeping penitent, crying for mercy. He was thoroughly and permanently converted.*

Thus passed a cheerful interview in reminiscences of the great men of our Israel, and anecdotes which are as marvelous instances of the grace of God as they are facetious examples of the ludicrous.

* These anecdotes, which, with many others of less credibility, are current among the Wesleyan Methodists, are well authenticated in Methodist records.

A MEDITATIVE HABIT

"Isaac went out to meditate in the field at eventide."
                                                    Moses

It was one of the philosophical rules of Pythagoras and his disciples to review, by close meditation, the events of each day. Cicero, though adhering to a different sect of philosophy, adopted the rule merely for its intellectual advantage. He found that it invigorated his memory—a faculty to which the ancients attached high importance. He tells us that he practiced the precept daily. The rule is infinitely more applicable to Christians. Summerfield was in the habit of selecting a text every morning as the theme of his meditations through the day—a point around which his thoughts could revolve at every interval of leisure, and to which he could summon them away from every casual, and especially every hurtful, suggestion of the senses or of the tempter.

The formation of a *meditative habit*—who can doubt its value to the Christian character? How entirely would it transform most professors of religion! What stability, and energy, and dignity, would it impart to their conduct! How much more profoundly would they comprehend and appreciate their religion!

Let me not be misunderstood. I do not mean merely a habit of *sobriety*, much less a moping ruminating reserve; but a habit of frequent, of daily meditation on the Scripture doctrines—of self-inspection, and of self-comparison with the Scripture standard of character—such a habit as every literary man finds it necessary to cultivate in respect to his intellectual improvement—close and frequent application to his books and his subjects—constant introspection.

Now, is not this one of the means by which Christianity is adapted to raise up the mass of the popular mind? Was Christianity designed to exert only an indirect agency in the intellectual elevation of man; to furnish nutriment for his heart, but not his mind? This is as far as the Christian world, it seems, has generally allowed its influence to extend; but it is a mistake. Its immediate purpose is the correction of the heart; but it is adapted and designed to raise up, by a direct application, the intellectual and the social condition of man. It is *the* instrument for the elevation of the total condition of the world. We are beginning to recognize this fact, and to make direct application of religious principles to individual social evils, as legalized intemperance, slavery, and war. Who doubts that the improvement of our minds is a moral duty of even higher obligation than the care of our health? Who doubts that the time will come when this point will be so clearly understood that the Christian, who unnecessarily neglects his mental cultivation, will be considered criminal; more criminal than if he should deliberately ruin his health by declining food? Alas! how novel, though reasonable, is such a thought at present! By intellectual improvement we do not mean here the cultivation of particular faculties, or the study of particular sciences, but that general enlargement and invigoration of the intellectual nature which should be the object of all mental discipline. Now, what we do say is, that *the popular influence of religion should have this effect. Wherever it is eminent it has this effect.* Who has not been struck by the strong good sense, the tranquil energy, the mental integrity and symmetry, which some persons seem to attain at once on receiving the blessing of sanctification? It sets them to *thinking*, and acting, as well as feeling. Who does not see in the character of the sacred oracles this adaptation of religion? How are they adorned with every attraction of intellect; how unparalleled their poetry; how profound their logic; how characteristic their biography; what substance for thought teems in every text! The antique records stand, in this late age, confessed, by friends and foes, to be unparalleled, in mere intellectual traits, among all the productions of the human mind.

If this is the tendency of Christianity, how can each individual bring it to bear on his own nature more effectually than by a *meditative habit?* Such a habit would promote our knowledge of religious truth. What an ample field does the Bible afford of "all delectable flowers and fruits!" Each doctrine is a golden vein, leading into the great mine of the whole. Now, if we should combine with our daily Scripture reading, daily meditation upon the truth we read, how would it deepen our spiritual knowledge! It is wonderful how ignorant most laymen are of the Christian doctrines. They have vague ideas of the essential ones; but how few of them can give clear statements of the nature of Faith, the Witness of the Spirit, the Atonement, the Trinity, &c.! It is a good thing that, in the experience of all Christians, these truths are indirectly involved; but it would be better if, in addition, they could be theoretically understood. God has not judged them unworthy of being revealed; we should not deem them unworthy of being studied. The habit we recommend would make us *Scriptural* Christians. The hallowed sentiments of the Scriptures would be more familiar to our minds, and their beautiful phraseology more common in our speech.

It would give greater decision and fixedness to the mind. By such a course we would test and estimate the grounds of our faith. We would be saved from the frequent misgivings which attend a desultory-minded Christian. Settled in our doctrines, we would be more uniform in our conduct, and more unwavering in our experience. We would act more from principle than impulse. Our whole being, as Christians, would become more vigorous and determinate. And from this state would result a more regular frame of feeling. Is it not the case that Christians, more than others, are subject to vicissitudes of feeling? It is not occasioned by their piety, but their weakness. How many caprices of feeling and useless anxieties would be prevented by enlarged views and fixed principles in religion! There is no Christian minister who has not met with cases of profound wretchedness occasioned by wrong views of Christian doctrine; and these views are frequently too inveterate to be corrected. They would have been prevented by a better knowledge of Scripture theology.

THE MARINER'S PREACHER.

"Was lost and is found."—Christ.

During the last war lived, in an obscure suburb of the city of B——, a poor but devoted English woman, who, having lost her husband soon after her emigration, depended for her subsistence on the earnings of her needle. Her neighbors were of the lowest class—ignorant and vicious. She felt, amid her poverty and toils, that God might have cast her lot in those unfavorable circumstances for some good purpose, and began zealously to plan for the religious improvement of the neighborhood. Among other means, she opened her little front room several times a week for a prayer meeting; and procured the aid of several pious Methodists in conducting it. Much of the good seed thus scattered with a faith that hoped against hope, and in a soil that seemed nothing but arid sand, produced good fruit; but I confine myself only to one instance, which, in its diversified results, can be fully estimated in eternity alone.

Among the attendants at the evening meeting was a young sailor, with an intellectual eye, a prepossessing countenance, and all the generous susceptibilities of a sailor's heart. Amid the corruptions of his associates he had been noted for his temperance and excellent disposition. And yet this child of the sea had been a wanderer on its waves from his earliest years. He could scarcely trace the tie of a single family relation on earth, and had known no other friends than the ever-varying but true-hearted companionship of the forecastle. A natural superiority of head and heart had, under the providence of God, raised him above many of the moral perils of his lot. His fine traits interested much the good English woman and her pious associates, and they could not see why God would not make some use of him among his comrades. He had received no education, but could read imperfectly. She hoped that God would in some way provide for his future instruction; but in the midst of her anticipations he was suddenly summoned away to sea. He had been out but a short time when the vessel was seized by a British privateer, and carried into Halifax, where the crew suffered a long and wretched imprisonment.

A year had passed away, during which the good woman had heard nothing of the young sailor. Her hopes of him were abandoned as extravagant, in view of his unsettled mode of life, and its peculiar impediments to all improvement. Still she remembered and prayed for him with the solicitude of a mother. About this time she received a letter from her relations who had settled in Halifax, on business which required her to visit that town. While there, her habitual disposition to be useful led her, with a few friends, to visit the prison with tracts. In one apartment were the American prisoners. As she approached the grated door a voice shouted her name, calling her mother, and a youth beckoned and leaped for joy at the grate: it was the lost sailor boy! They wept and conversed like mother and son; and when she left she gave him a Bible, his future guide and comfort.

During her stay at Halifax she constantly visited the prison, supplying the youth with tracts, religious books, and clothing; and endeavoring, by her conversation, to secure the religious impressions made on his mind by the prayer meetings in B——. After some months she removed to a distant part of the provinces, and for years she heard nothing more of the young sailor.

* * * * * *

In 18— I was appointed to B——. One of the most agreeable circumstances of this new appointment was, that it afforded me the acquaintance of "Father T.," the celebrated mariner's preacher of the city—a gentleman whose fame for genius and usefulness was general; whose extraordinary character has been sketched in our periodicals, and the books of transatlantic visitors,* as one of the so-called "lions" of the city, whom a distinguished critic has pronounced the greatest poet of the land, though unable to write a stanza; and the mayor of B—— had publicly declared a more effectual protector of the peace of the most degraded parts of the city than any hundred policemen.

In the spacious and substantial chapel, crowded about by the worst habitations of the city, this distinguished man delivered, every sabbath, discourses the most extraordinary, to assemblies also as extraordinary, perhaps, as are to be found in the Christian world. In the centre column of seats, guarded sacredly against all other intrusion, sat a dense mass of mariners—a strange medley of white, black, and olive—Protestant, Catholic, and pagan—representing many languages, unable, it may be, to comprehend each other's vocal speech, but speaking there the same language of intense looks and flowing

* See Miss Martineau, Buckingham, and, more recently, Dickens.

tears. On the other seats, in the galleries, the aisles, the altar, and on the pulpit stairs, crowded, week after week, and year after year, with the families of sailors, and the poor who had no other temple, the elite of the city—the learned professor, the student, the popular writer, the actor, groups of clergymen, and the votaries of gayety and fashion—listening with throbbing hearts and wet eyes to a man whose only school had been the forecastle, whose only endowments those of grace and nature; but whose discourses presented the strongest, the most brilliant exhibition I have ever witnessed, of shrewd sense, epigrammatic thought, melting pathos, and resistless humor, expressed in a style of pertinency, spangled over by an exhaustless variety of the finest images, and pervaded by a spiritual earnestness that subdued all listeners—a man who could scarcely speak three sentences in the pulpit, or out of it, without presenting a striking poetical image, a phrase of rare beauty, or a sententious sarcasm, and the living examples of whose usefulness are scattered over the seas.

* * * * * * **

During my second year in B——, an aged English local preacher moved to the city from the British provinces, and became connected with my charge. His wife, though advanced in years, had that colloquial vivacity, motherly affectionateness, and air of tidiness, which we often find in the better-trained women of the common people of England. I felt a cordial comfortableness about their humble hearth which was not to be found in more stately dwellings, and often resorted to it for an hour of sociability and conversation. I thus became acquainted with her history—her former residence in the city—the evening prayer meeting—her removal to the provinces—her second marriage, etc.

* * * * * *

The old local preacher was mingling in a public throng one day with a friend, when they met "Father T." A few words of introduction led to a free conversation in which the former residence of his wife in the city was mentioned; an allusion was made to her prayer meeting—her former name was asked by "Father T." He seemed seized by an impulse; inquired their residence; hastened away, and in a short time arrived in a carriage, with all his family, at the home of the aged pair. There a scene ensued which I must leave to the imagination of the reader. "Father T." was the sailor boy of the prayer meeting and the prison; the old

2

lady was the widow who had first cared for his soul. They had met once more!

Her husband has since gone to heaven; and she resides in humble but comfortable obscurity, unknown to the world, but exerting upon it, through the sailor preacher, an influence for good which the final day alone can fully reveal.

Reader, there may be a neglected spirit within thy reach, which, reclaimed by thine influence from vice, might be to thee an agency of inestimable usefulness; a gem on the brow of the church on earth, and a blessed companion in thy walks over the "flowery meads" of heaven. Under the abject rags of poverty is wrapped a jewel which may glitter on the crown of the Redeemer in the heavens; and which an archangel would descend swiftly from the skies to seize and recover. But to angels is denied this honor; yet it may be thine! and it may afford thee more "riches of glory" than could all the diadems of earth.

2

UTILITY OF SABBATH SCHOOLS.

'All thy children shall be taught of the Lord, and great shall be the peace of thy children."—Isaiah.

Would that I could place every child of this land in a sabbath school. I should prefer this usefulness to that of the " father of his country." I should thereby secure and aggrandize its destiny more than all treasures, and arms, and legislation could; nay, it would thus be made the light of the world! I wish to put on record an humble word for this noble institution.

Among the distinguishing advantages of the sabbath school, I consider most important—

Its tendency to counteract the almost universal mis-education of the moral character of children. The only system of education which is sanctioned by the spirit and principles of Christianity, is that which is based on the recognition of man's eternity ; which calculates, as its first object, the improvement of his heart; and teaches him to estimate everything else only as it is subservient to the world to come. . How widely different is this from the prevailing systems of education! How seldom is the young immor tal impressed with the admonition, that all its present improvements should be made in reference to the eternal future! Its calculations are limited to the present world. The first and chief incentive addressed to its mind is one that appeals to the most depraved affection of our fallen nature—*selfishness*. It is exhorted to diligence in its improvement for its own aggrandizement. Its infant hands may indeed be clasped, and its young voice taught, morning and evening, to say—" Our Father, who art in heaven ;" but it is too frequently only because of the lovely simplicity of the act. Religion is made too much a matter of mere incidental attention, fit only for the leisure of a sabbath day, for a sick bed, or a dying hour. The instructions of the sabbath school tend to counteract this defective training. They point the young mind to its future state—a state where its present actions will be developing their result when suns have quenched their fires and the stars have fallen from heaven.

From the consideration of the influence of the sabbath school on personal character, the transition is natural to its influence on the public character of communities. The character of a community is but a combination of the more prominent and general traits that mark the personal character of the individuals who compose it. Hence one is a more or less true criterion of the other; they are as inseparably connected as cause and effect. Wherever, therefore, any average standard of individual character can be introduced in a community, that will be the standard of its public character. The sabbath school, acting, as it does, on so large a mass of the community, and that, too, in the most susceptible time of life, must exert an important influence on its character. The salutary tendency of religious knowledge has been attested in the history of every community where the experiment has been made. In Ireland, a country affording sufficient natural facilities for every comfort and refinement, the universal features of society are beggary, grossness, and superstition; while in Scotland, a land far less favorable in soil and climate, in the lowliest cottage dwell neatness and social virtue. "The disparity," says one who is competent to judge, (Robert Hall,) "can be ascribed only to the difference of moral and mental cultivation in the two places." Ireland is depressed under the influence of a degrading religion, which precludes the Bible from her children, and substitutes in its place a medley of demoralizing errors; Scotland is blessed with an evangelical faith, and an enlightened clergy; and has been taught to consider her beautiful and romantic scenery deficient without the additional ornament of the school-house and the church spire

South America is darkened with superstition, corrupt with vice, and rent with political anarchy. *New-England* is the oasis of the world, the light of knowledge illuminates the cradle shines around the hearth, irradiates the work shop, and blends with all the intercourses of social life. Peace and quiet pervade its extent. *South America* has been for ages under the influence of a corrupt hierarchy, whose motto, asserted in theory, and carried out in practice, is, that "ignorance is the mother of devotion." *New-England*, on the other hand, was settled by men who reposed their hopes for the well-being of their posterity on the power of education and religion; who, in their patriarchal simplicity, gathered together their rusty books to found a college library; gave the produce of their harvests, by the bushel, from their garners, for the subsistence of its faculty; and who, rather than be without the district school-house, would, every man of them, take a beam from his cottage with which to build one.

The morality of the Bible furnishes the only sure basis for any good social order. It has given to our own land its moral elevation. It has ornamented its towns and villages with the church spire, pointing to the God of our fathers; and the humming school-house, the sanctuary of our children—it has spread peace and competence through our community, and brought comfort and endearment to our homes. The Bible was the boast of our fathers: under its sanction they fought the battles of our liberty; on its principles they founded our institutions. They were not deluded;—the results attest their wisdom.

The Sunday school is an efficient instrumentality for suppressing vice and calling out latent intellect, from its adaptation to the poor. It is particularly important to the children of the poor, because they are, from their circumstances and the examples around them, exposed to vice. Their parents are necessarily engaged in labor, and cannot devote proper attention to their training. As soon as they are able to engage in manual work they must leave the public school, and, without the sabbath school, be destitute of the means of mental improvement—left to grow up in ignorance and vice, and become the paupers and criminals of the community. Among the poor are frequently the best materials for usefulness and greatness. It is the testimony of all literary biography, that the elements of intellectual greatness are chiefly to be found among the obscure. Uneffeminated, accustomed to scenes of self-dependence, cradled in poverty, and nursed on the marble bosom of adversity, they possess that true masculineness and energy that fit the mind for high purposes and great emergencies. There is too much truth in the remark of the poet,—

" Full many a gem, of purest ray serene,
　The dark unfathom'd caves of ocean bear;
　Full many a flower is born to blush unseen,
　And waste its sweetness on the desert air."

And in the grave-yard of many an obscure village molders, with the ashes of peasants and plough-boys, the unhonored remains of those

" Whose hearts were pregnant with celestial fire·
　Whose hands the rod of empire might have sway'd.
　Or waked to ecstasy the living lyre."

Original greatness of mind, such as, under the education of Newton, made the author of the " Principia," or, under the circumstances of Milton, made the author of " Paradise Lost," is not local in its distribution. It may reside in the cranium of the peasant, the mechanic, or the tar, as well as in that of the occupant of the college domicil. But, in the one case it is called out, in the other it is not; thus many a latent spark of intellectual fire has gone out which might have kindled into a beacon light to guide a nation or an age. The sabbath school furnishes us with access to such minds. Who can estimate the amount of mental energy it is putting into operation, the pearls it is bringing up from the depths of obscurity?

Again, contemplate its probable influence on the future character of the Christian church, both laity and ministry. It is a truth which all observation has rendered familiar, that the earliest impressions of the mind are the most powerful, and are of the utmost moment in the development of the subsequent character. Hence the great importance everywhere attached to the early education of children—hence, the character of an adult is almost always a true criterion of his early training; and the intelligence and public virtue of a community are a sure index to its state of primary education. So that the fact now alluded to applies, not only to individual character, but to the public character of communities, which, as above said, is but the aggregate of individual character.

Now, with this important fact, taught us by the whole history of human nature, what calculations may we not make in regard to the future influence of this institution on the Christian church, and on the whole moral world? It brings the regenerating influences of the gospel to operate on the first moral susceptibilities of the young immortal spirit; it blends these influences with the unperverted sympathies and tender affections of childhood. It directs its soft rays on the budding flower. And there is a purity in the first and fresh affections of the young heart—a purity which we all remember, but which the searing influence of later years too often and too fatally perverts—that is congenial with the influences of the gospel, and secures to them a much more promising effect than in later years. If early training has so remarkable an influence on the character of individuals and communities, we may well presume that, when the sabbath school shall have accomplished the full experiment of its influence, it will exhibit results, the anticipations of which should send gladness and hope through the Christian world. That experiment has not yet been completed; it has been but partially prosecuted. A single generation has not yet passed since the general establishment of the institution. Indeed, the experiment is not yet fully *commenced*. The sabbath school has hardly yet attained a general establishment, even in the Christian world. And yet already it has been productive of the most gratifying results; wherever it is in operation it is training up a new generation of Christians—men and women disciplined, almost from their cradle-days, to the duties and enterprises of religion, with souls baptized into its spirit, and active with its strenuous energies. Who are they who make up the gross membership of our churches, and are most active in all their enterprises? Are they the aged—the middle-aged? There are indeed a few of the former, the elders of Israel, who give venerable counsel in the gates of the city, and more of the latter; but it is confessed that the efficiency of the American church is now in the hands of her young men and young women —those who have entered its pale since the epoch of sabbath schools.

This was not the case in the days of the fathers. Youthful piety was then a remarkable circumstance. Youthful morality was indeed common, but not piety—the provisions of the times were just sufficient to impose the restraints of morality, which were expected, in mature years, to strengthen into piety. But now our congregations are thronged with the young. Our altars are bedewed with the penitent tears of youth and childhood. Juvenile piety is infusing spirit and vivacity into all the movements of Christendom; and the strong energy of young manhood has laid hold, in its might, upon the cross, and is redeeming the world, and sending trembling through the ranks of darkness and error. Who can doubt that the sabbath school has had an important agency in producing that spirit of moral enterprise which, since the date of this institution, but not before, has revived the church into life, and filled the civilized world with moral activity?

And what effect is this institution having and is it destined to have on the *ministry?* How many hundreds, who now stand prominently in its ranks, and thousands who are preparing to stand there, have received their first impressions of the truth, and their commission to preach it, through the faithful sabbath-school teacher? It is the theological school of the millennium! From it are to go forth those master spirits who will be demanded by the future emergencies of the church, and who alone will be competent to conduct its final triumphs—the men whose strong arms are to hold up her ensigns in the last battles, and bear them on before a yielding world—men who, like the youth of the best days of the classic nations, shall have been trained and hardened for the work from infancy—self-sacrificing men, who will throw their whole souls and bodies into every exigency of the church, and, like

Leonidas and his Spartans, guard the moral passes of the world against the enemy. Such men are wanted by the present openings for the spread of the gospel; and we cannot but think that Providence has brought into being this institution, as a wisely-adapted means of meeting this necessity of the times.

Lastly, this institution appears interesting to me as a beautiful example of that sympathy and attentiveness for the well-being of all men which the Christian spirit inspires. It brings the light of eternity down to the very cradle. It sweetens the loveliness of childhood with the sanctifying influences of the gospel. It imparts the cheering comforts of those blessed doctrines which teach us the saving love of the Redeemer, the parental superintendence of our heavenly Father, and the hope of a peaceful heaven, where sorrowing and sighing shall flee away, and the hand of God shall wipe tears from all eyes, to the first anxieties of the dawning and inquisitive mind. Instead of allowing those passions which deprave and imbitter the heart to grow, until they become fixed habits, binding the soul as with shackles of brass, it seeks to eradicate them in their first germination. It illuminates the smiles of unperverted childhood with the loveliness of infant piety, and throws around wayward youth the strong shield of religious principle. It exposes not, like infidelity, these lambs of the flock to every beast of prey that prowls to despoil them of their innocence; but, like an imbodied angel, it takes them to its arms, as did the Saviour of the world, and blesses them: " Of such is the kingdom of heaven." They are the emblems of the innocence of the skies; under the training of the sabbath school they become the cherubs of the earthly church.

I lately heard a discourse in behalf of this institution in which the preacher spoke emphatically of the adaptation of the sabbath school to rescue the exposed children of the poor, and concluded with an illustrative anecdote which took the assembly by surprise. Twelve years ago, said he, there lived, not one mile from this spot, in a solitary chamber, a poor widow and her four children, the oldest three of whom had but imperfectly learned to read. They had seen happier days; but the father of the family died after a protracted illness, which consumed all their resources. The widow gathered her little ones into a small house, and by toiling day and night with her needle, and month after month, selling articles of their former furniture, sustained them a few years. Her labor, which was continued often till near the dawn of day, destroyed health, and prostrated her with pulmonary consumption, under which she languished through two or three years. During this time her eldest daughter had to attend her sick bed, and the suffering family depended entirely on the labors of two sons, (the eldest not twelve years of age,) in a neighboring factory. The charity of their poor neighbors sometimes relieved them; but often were they reduced to bread or potatoes alone for food, and a few chips for their comfortless hearth. They were crowded at last into a single room, where the heart-broken mother soon died, hoping in God for a rest beyond the grave, and leaving to his protection her helpless children.

Three of these children had, in former years, and, occasionally, during their sad afflictions, attended a sabbath school, which was established for the benefit of the poor in the neighborhood, and superintended by an humble but devoted blacksmith. At the decease of their mother, the two sisters and younger brother were placed in distant situations, while the eldest boy continued to work in the factory, and attend the sabbath school. The death of his mother prepared his heart for religious impressions. In a few months he was converted to God in a class meeting of children connected with the school. And now the spirit within him was roused to exertion; he took the library books of the school in his pocket to the factory, tied them open on the posts of his room, and at every leisure moment snatched a few lines of reading: thus he toiled on, serving God and improving his mind, till some liberal Christians rescued him from his lowly lot, and sent him to school, and in time he became a preacher of the word of life. While at school he received the joyful tidings of his eldest sister's conversion; and she is now a devoted member of the church. His younger brother had been placed in the country several miles from any church, and amid influences which hardly allowed the hope of his being awakened and converted. Yet the former impressions of the sabbath school remained. The divine Spirit enforced them, and he was, by and by, led to the distant house of God; he became converted, and is now also in the ministry.

Thus were these three saved, under the most unpropitious circumstances, by at least the indirect instrumentality of this valuable institution. And why were they thus discriminated from the younger child, who still remains unconverted? There is no answer, except that from her early age at that time, and unfavorable circumstances since, she has never come under the influence of the sabbath school. The oldest son has recently been traveling abroad; and, from the scenes of trans-atlantic art and romance, he has returned with the yearning heart of a pilgrim approaching his holy shrine, to look once more on the old school-room where he received all his hopes, and to shake the hardy hand of the Christian blacksmith who first directed his feet heavenward: and here that Sunday scholar stands before you to-night. The effect of this scene was deepened by the fact that two other young ministers sat in the pulpit at the time, who had been converted at the same school, and many of the most active members of the church had been scholars.

THE END

www.ingramcontent.com/pod-product-compliance
Lightning Source LLC
Chambersburg PA
CBHW020224240426
43672CB00006B/405